10/01

D0908153

Paths of Faith

Paths of Faith

Conversations About Religion and Spirituality

MICHAEL THOMAS FORD

Simon & Schuster Books for Young Readers
New York   London   Toronto   Sydney   Singapore

SIMON & SCHUSTER BOOKS FOR YOUNG READERS

An imprint of Simon & Schuster Children's Publishing Division

1230 Avenue of the Americas, New York, New York 10020

Copyright © 2000 by Michael Thomas Ford

All rights reserved including the right of reproduction

in whole or in part in any form.

SIMON & SCHUSTER BOOKS FOR YOUNG READERS

is a trademark of Simon & Schuster.

Book design by Steve Scott

The text of this book is set in Weiss.

Printed and bound in the United States of America

2 4 6 8 10 9 7 5 3 1

CIP Data for this book is available from the Library of Congress.

ISBN 0-689-82263-4

Acknowledgments

This book would never have come together were it not for the women and men who took time to speak with me and offer their experiences to readers. Without you, there would be no book at all. I am also thankful for the help of the many people who guided me to interview subjects, recommended their favorite books, and provided advice along the way, in particular the Reverend Paul Zahl, Peggy Morscheck, Tamar Ellentuck, Dan Sokatch, Lynn Stone, Stephen Shutt, and Joe Bruchac. And finally, my deepest appreciation to my friends of the Green Men circle, who add so much to my life and make walking the path a challenge and a joy.

Contents

Author's Note

There are as many different ways of expressing religious faith and spirituality as there are people in the world. The purpose of this book is to show you how a handful of people do just that. It would be impossible to include in one book representatives from every religion, or even to discuss what the different groups within each religion believe. The eleven people whose stories are included here come from a variety of religious traditions. But while they may be members of a particular religion, they speak only for themselves. They tell their personal stories, not the stories of anyone else in their tradition, or even the stories of the traditions themselves.

Each interview begins with a brief overview of the religion being discussed, but this is not intended as a book to explain the history and beliefs of any religion. In fact, you'll find that some of the people included here don't always agree with the traditional beliefs of their religion. Instead, each interview is meant to show how one person living and expressing spirituality within a tradition has done that, and what the joys and challenges of living in that tradition have been. If you wish to find out more about a particular religion discussed in the book, there are sources of additional information listed at the end of each interview.

Some of the people in this book may come from the same tradition that you yourself do. Others may come from traditions you have never even heard of. You might agree with some of the things that are said, and you might disagree with some of them. As you read these stories try to keep in mind that these are the personal, individual stories of people who have spent a large part of their lives living, working, and celebrating within particular religions and spiritual traditions. Hear what each of them has to say. See what each of them has in common, what makes each of them unique, and how your own beliefs compare. Think of this book as a beginning, a place to start exploring how different kinds of people celebrate the many voices of the spirit.

Michael Thomas Ford

John Cardinal O'Connor

Former Archbishop, the Catholic Diocese of New York

"My job is to try to know and love and serve God. That means knowing and loving and serving his people, and hoping that I will end up in heaven when it's all over. That's what life is about."

Roman Catholicism is the largest of the Christian traditions, and thereby the largest of the world's religious traditions. The word *catholic* is Greek for "universal," and the name reflects the basic belief of the Roman Catholic faith, which is that Jesus Christ (circa 7 B.C.–A.D. 30), whom Catholics believe is the Son of God, was sent to Earth to save all of humankind from eternal damnation.

What is factually known about Jesus is that he was a Jew whose teachings about how to live an ethical life and achieve eternal salvation attracted a strong following. Because of his teachings, Christ was killed by crucifixion by the Roman government. Catholics believe that

1

Christ was resurrected from the dead three days after his death, and that he then ascended to heaven to be with God. Because of his birth, life, and death, they believe, those who follow the teachings of Christ and the church he founded will also be taken to heaven to live with God when they die.

Catholics, like all Christians, see the Bible, particularly the New Testament, as containing the teachings of Jesus Christ and the story of his life and works. The central focus of Catholic worship is the Mass, a service that recalls the life of Christ and remembers his sacrificial death in the form of Holy Communion.

Church doctrine teaches that before his death Christ appointed one of his apostles, Peter, as the head of the Christian Church, making him the first pope, or father, of the church. Peter then appointed other church leaders as bishops, who in turn handed down control of the church, and this line of succession is believed to continue unbroken today. The current head of the Roman Catholic Church is His Holiness Pope John Paul II, who resides in the seat of the church at the Vatican in Rome.

In the United States one of the most respected and influential leaders of the Roman Catholic Church was John Cardinal O'Connor, the archbishop of the diocese of New York who passed away several months after this interview was conducted. Cardinal O'Connor was born and raised in Philadelphia. He was ordained in 1945 to the Roman Catholic priesthood, and has studied at a

Paths of Faith

number of colleges and universities. He holds advanced degrees in ethics, clinical psychology, and political theory.

After doing teaching and parish work in Philadelphia, Cardinal O'Connor worked as a chaplain with the United States Navy and the Marine Corps, serving for twenty-seven years. Upon leaving military service, he was ordained a bishop for the armed forces of the United States by Pope John Paul II in 1979. In 1983 he became the bishop of Scranton, Pennsylvania, and in 1984, the archbishop of New York. He was created a cardinal in 1985 and served until his death in May 2000.

You were ordained a priest in 1945, as a very young man. What led you to the priesthood?

I was fortunate to come from a very simple Catholic family. We lived in a little row house in Philadelphia, and my father worked with his hands, as a gold leafer. We went very faithfully to Mass on Sundays. But there was never any push in our family to go into any particular vocation. It came as a surprise to my mother and father when I told them that I wanted to enter the seminary. My father had expected me to work with him when I got out of school, but he agreed that if this was what I wanted to do, then it was what I should do.

There were no great revelations, no lightning bolts from heaven. It was a quiet kind of thing. I think it was the result of the simple kind of family life I had, coupled with the fact that when I went to West Catholic High School in Philadelphia, I was taught by the La Salle Christian Brothers, who were tremendously influential in fostering vocations to the religious life. I think that their influence was very helpful to me. But that was about it.

Originally I wanted to be a so-called missionary priest. When I was in high school, they had vocation days, which featured literature from a lot of different religious communities. I was entranced by pictures of places like Mount Kilimanjaro in Africa, and most particularly by pictures of the Maryknoll Missions in China. So I went to the parish priest with stars in my eyes about the foreign missions, but he urged me instead to go to the seminary.

You were ordained a priest right at the end of World War II, and you were later a naval chaplain for the U.S. Navy and the Marine Corps. Did seeing the effects of war have a profound effect on your spiritual life?

I spent twenty-seven years in the navy and Marine Corps, serving pretty much all over the world. I would say that it very definitely had a strong impact on my spiritual life. In a certain sense the priest *is* the church wherever he goes in the military. He is more often than not alone, sometimes thousands of miles away from any other priest or any of the structures that we are accustomed to. He has to hold on to a prayer life. He has to say Mass every day. He has to pray his rosary.

It is a strengthening period. For example, many a night at sea I would invite a group of men up on deck with a hundred billion stars out there, and we'd look at the wake of the ship as we were churning through the waters and pray the rosary together. That's a very strengthening influence. Combat is a very strengthening influence. Once again, you have no immediate priest associates or the structures of the church. Your men are in danger and you're in danger at any time. In my case, I lived in a hole in the ground in Vietnam with the mud and the rain, or in a tent. A tent was luxurious compared to the hole. I never knew what was going to happen. Sometimes we were out in areas where every twig that snapped could be approaching death. At those times either you throw everything overboard or you develop a much more intense and highly personalized spiritual life.

How do you personally see your connection to God, and how does that relationship affect your own life?

It is a very, very personal thing. I never feel that God is very far away. I talk with him on a personal basis. I think of God primarily as our Lord—as Christ—because he became a human being. He is someone I walk with and talk with and turn to. I feel his presence at all times.

John Cardinal O'Connor   5

To me, this is of immense importance. I need to have that personal sense of Christ with me at all times, particularly in the Eucharist and in celebrating Mass. When I visit a chapel or church, I know that Christ is just as truly present there as he was present in the womb of Mary or on the cross, and simultaneously he is very personally present with me wherever I go. If I didn't have that, I think that I would be in very deep trouble. And on those occasions when I feel depressed, discouraged, or lonely—and anyone who doesn't experience such moments is, I think, probably a robot—the intellectual awareness of God's presence, but mostly the personal, spiritual, and emotional awareness, is what keeps me going.

Over the years have you ever had moments when you've doubted aspects of the Catholic tradition or what you believe?

Not the Catholic tradition as such. The most difficult period of my life hit me very suddenly and unexpectedly. I was in Okinawa, in the middle of the Pacific Ocean, with a huge marine unit. I was thousands of miles from home. Without warning, I was hit with an emptiness, a sense of desolation and a questioning of everything. We had a little chapel, a very crude metal hut. I would go in at night after the base was pretty still, and I would kneel there. I would cry. I would be silent. I would internally scream out, asking where God was. I would ask myself if he was really there, present in the

Paths of Faith

Blessed Sacrament, something I had never questioned before in my life. For a period of perhaps three months this went on. I did my job every day. I said Mass. I worked with the troops. I sat all day and listened to their problems. I worked with command.

Then the time came to prepare to go to Vietnam, into the unknown, and I did my best to help everyone else. This was a period I discussed with no one. No one knew what was going on inside me. All I could do was keep reminding myself over and over of our Lord's words on the cross, where he cried out, "My God, my God, why have you forsaken me?"

And then it left as rapidly as it came, after about three months. It has never returned. I think my faith, and my sense of the personal presence of Christ, were deepened tremendously by that, even though I was hanging on by my fingernails. It was an experience I would never want to go through again, but it is an experience I never regret, because I think it not only deepened my own faith, but gave me a much, much deeper sensitivity to, and empathy with, people who have no faith at all, people who feel abandoned, people who feel lost, people who just don't know which way to turn and live in darkness. I don't ever regret it and I am grateful for it, but once is enough.

You've given up a lot of the things that many people have in their lives—marriage, children, a career based on wealth and worldly success. Do you ever wonder what your life might have been like if you had not entered the priesthood?

I probably would have been a bricklayer or a truck driver. I have no illusions about that. The church gave me a magnificent education and made an education possible for me. The church has made me whatever I am today. I am in an extraordinarily visible position at this time in my life as the archbishop of one of the best-known archdioceses in the world, the archdiocese of New York, and it would have been utterly preposterous for me ever to dream of reaching this point of visibility or of being treated as I am treated. I have no pretensions about myself at all, or about how I got where I am. It's all due to the church and to the people who helped me along the way.

In my latter years in the seminary the worst war that the world has ever known—World War II—was raging. All my associates of my age were being drafted. Had I not been in the seminary, I would have been drafted myself, or felt the patriotic duty to join the military. I might well have been killed in World War II, as were many of the men my age. Certainly my life would have been radically different. There were five children in my family. One died, and of the four living, I was the only one who went to college and got an education. That was because of the church.

I think it's very important for all of us to remember

that the sacrifices that parents make, the sacrifices that a lot of other people in our life make, make our own life possible. In my case, there were many, many people who made it possible for me to get the education that I got, to be given the positions that I was given, to be able to serve twenty-seven years in the United States Navy and the Marine Corps. I wouldn't have had any of this. This has all been a gift given to me by God, and by others. This is much more true of people who reach lofty positions in the world, and I'm afraid many of them never recognize it or admit it. I don't care whether you're a highly successful surgeon, businessperson, actor, or anything else. If someone has achieved anything, if someone is in a prominent position or a position of authority or wealth, where would he or she be if a tremendous number of people hadn't contributed to his or her achievement? Maybe a humble teacher in an elementary school or a caring teacher in a high school encouraged him or her. I think many of us tend to take ourselves far too seriously. That can happen to a cardinal archbishop as well if he doesn't keep reminding himself of his roots.

But do you ever miss any of the things you could have had, like children or a relationship with someone else?

I think that most people want to get married, and most people want to have children and have their own family and their own constant companion and someone to turn to. The priesthood can be a very, very lonely life. The position of the cardinal archbishop of New York can be an indescribably lonely life. So sure, I think about what might have been. But I can't really imagine it. As I said before, I think my life would have been determined in large measure by the circumstances of where I was born and raised, and by World War II and subsequent wars. So even when I think about what might have been, or of what I might have done, I have to recognize that the probability of my having reached a position comparable to what God has given me in the church would have been very, very remote.

Do you ever have moments when you wish you could just call up one of your friends and go to a movie or a baseball game?

The last time I was in a movie theater was, I think, about twenty-eight years ago. I saw *The Last Days of Hitler*. I remember that very clearly.

That's not a very cheery film to have as your last movie.

No, it wasn't. Maybe that's why I haven't gone since. But yes, I do wish I could. I would settle for simply being able to get into some old clothes and take a walk down Fifth Avenue in New York. But you do what you're supposed to do, in accordance with your particular

Paths of Faith

responsibilities in life. People here expect to see me in my black suit and Roman collar, or in a cassock or the vestments that I wear in church. Saint Paul says that every high priest is taken from among men for the things that pertain to God. So even though I am very much one with the people—and I think an awful lot of people in New York know that—at the same time I am not an immediate member of a family. I am not one who can simply go out and walk the streets as anybody else can.

Do you ever feel that you are able to get away from all the responsibility and be just John, instead of John Cardinal O'Connor, archbishop of New York?

It's very hard. I don't know if I made a conscious decision at some point or if it just happened and became evident to me, but I just belong to the people. And that's not said to be noble. You simply cannot be the archbishop of New York and decide that you have a private life and a right to live a private life. I belong to the people here. I belong to the Jewish people here, to the Muslim people here, to the Protestant people here, to the Catholic people here. That's what's expected of the archbishop of New York, or at least the way that I see the job. I am on the go from early morning to late at night. Pretty much the only time that I am alone, except for saying my prayers, is when I go to bed at the end of the day.

John Cardinal O'Connor

I honestly don't believe that I have a right to a private life. Certainly I don't have a right to a private morality, to do as I please. I belong to the community, and the community expects certain things of me, certain standards of me. The people have a right, as I see it, to get mad at me. They have a right to be very, very demanding. This is a highly public life by nature. I can't speak of people in other positions. I am speaking very explicitly of my position.

Were you prepared for that kind of life before you became the archbishop of New York?

New York is a very different place. It's different from any place I've ever been before. But I am accustomed to living this life. You can't spend twenty-seven years in military service without living a very open life. When you're at sea, for instance, you are as seasick as everybody else. There is absolutely no privacy. When you're living with the marines in a hole in the ground, you're just like everybody else. Yet they still expect you to be a man of God. They expect you to be one with them, but different from them. They expect an added dimension. They don't expect you to be subject to the same things they are. If, for example, they fall into various temptations, they don't expect you to fall into them, but they expect you to understand their feelings. They expect you to understand sinfulness, to be sympathetic with it and not be condemning of it. Your life is truly, in the most literal sense, an open book. So from that perspective, at least, I was prepared to become the archbishop of New York.

Do you think that it's fair for people to expect you to understand some of the things they go through or feel, but not want you to feel them yourself?

They may recognize that you might have such feelings, but they don't expect you to succumb to them. I sometimes tell my brother bishops that being the archbishop of New York, you have to expect that even when you're changing your socks at some time during the day, there could be a camera catching it all on film. This is just a different place and a different life, and I've given myself over to that. I think most people know that I am available. They'll see me on the street and stop to say hello. They'll stop at the office or come to the house, and they expect me to be here for them. And not just Catholic people. People of many faiths speak of me as "their" archbishop, meaning that I belong to this city and this community. There is only one Roman Catholic archbishop of New York at any given time, and right now I'm it.

Because of your position as a spokesperson for the Catholic Church and for its beliefs, you have often been at the center of conflict and

John Cardinal O'Connor   13 *controversy because people have not agreed with or liked what you've said. How do you handle these moments?*

A fundamental maxim for me comes right from the Scriptures. It says that the disciple can't be greater than the master. Christ loved everybody. Christ did everything he could for everybody. And they responded by crucifying him. They spit at him and they screamed at him, and still he loved them. You can't do any more than that.

There is a basic psychological formula that says that frustration equals aggression. When people are frustrated, they become aggressive and angry, unless you can consciously resolve it in some way. So I tell my priests, when you're frustrated, don't scream at the people. Don't take it out on yourselves. Take it out on me. That's what I'm here for. And I really mean that. I know there are a lot of angry people in New York, and in the world, and better to have them angry at me than tearing themselves apart. It's better they take it out on me than on their husbands or their wives or anybody else.

What do you hope and believe will be the result of your lifetime spent serving God and the church?

I was raised in the old catechism, in which we asked the simple question, "Why did God make me?" And the answer is, "God made me to know him, to love him, and to serve him in this world and to be happy with him forever in the next." It's a very simple definition of life for me, and it's what I totally believe. I hope that I will get to heaven. I have no pretensions beyond that. I am too busy trying to do what I am expected to do now. I am not interested in postmortem monuments. The day will come, and maybe soon, when I will be in a crypt under the high altar of Saint Patrick's Cathedral. If anybody remembers that I was the archbishop of New York, that's fine. If nobody remembers, that's fine. My job is to try to know and love and serve God. That means knowing and loving and serving his people, and hoping that I will end up in heaven when it's all over. That's what life is about. That's what I was taught as a little kid. It's what my father and mother believed, and it's what they taught me from my earliest days. For me, that's it.

What, for you, has been the most rewarding part of a lifetime spent in service to the church?

That's pretty difficult to answer, because I have been so blessed in being a priest for more than fifty years now. I have no regrets about my years of military service or about my years of working for the church. There are highs and lows every day, every week, every year. For me, there is nothing at all comparable to being able to offer the sacrifice of the Mass. From that perspective, when I'm doing that, every day is a high point. I said the

Mass this morning, for example, and just being with the people and offering Mass with the people is a blessing. Every Sunday I am in Saint Patrick's Cathedral, and usually it's packed. It's very thrilling to me.

On the flip side of that question, what has been the most difficult part of a lifetime spent in service to the church?

That's easy. Paperwork, paperwork, paperwork. Dealing with finances. Trying to keep our schools open. Trying to keep our Catholic hospitals open. There's no question about what's the most difficult part. Every day I am begging. I beg from people of every religious persuasion and every ethnic background to help keep our Catholic schools open, because I passionately believe in them. To keep our Catholic hospitals open so that we can continue to do the social work of the gospel. This is, to me, very distasteful personally. But it has to be done. I would wish nothing greater for the next archbishop of New York than that he never have to see another piece of paper or have to think about money.

At this time it seems that more and more young people are returning to spirituality. What advice do you have for young people who might be exploring their own spirituality and trying to find their own way?

I would say to every young person what Saint Benedict said to his sister, who was to become Saint

Scholastica: Be a saint. Be yourself. You have to be authentic. Don't be fooled by the culture. Don't be overcome by what Pope John Paul II has called "the culture of death." It is pervasive. It eats like a cancer into our very being. Just be yourself. God made you essentially a wonderful, wonderful person, and to be yourself is to actualize the full potential of the person that God made you to be. The world crowds in on us. The world offers us absolutely crazy values. To be authentic, to be yourself, is a tough proposition. But it's more than worth it to actualize the potential that God has offered you. That's really to be a saint, to be yourself. Don't be the fraud that the world would demand that you be.

FOR MORE INFORMATION

ON-LINE RESOURCES

Catholic Information Center on the Internet
www.catholic.net

Catholic Online
www.catholic.org

Both of the above Web sites are great places to start for information about the Catholic Church. They provide contact information for numerous Catholic organizations, as well as links to other sites.

The Holy See: The Official Vatican Web Site
www.vatican.va

The Vatican is the official seat of the Catholic Church, and this fun Web site provides not only information on the history of the Vatican and its many historical sights, but also a lot of material on church doctrine and the latest news about the Pope's activities.

BOOKS

A Concise History of the Catholic Church, by Thomas S. Bokenkotter (Image Books, 1990). This critically acclaimed history covers the events and doctrines that have shaped Catholic thought and action over the past two thousand years.

Why Do Catholics Do That? A Guide to the Teachings and Practices of the Catholic Church, by Kevin Orlin Johnson (Ballantine, 1995). Written by a scholar and religion columnist, this book answers the most frequently asked questions on Catholic faith, worship, culture, and customs, including explanations of how the church makes its laws, the purpose of the sacraments, the origins of the Bible, the significance of the Blessed Virgin, the hierarchy of the Catholic clergy, and more.

The Seven Storey Mountain, by Thomas Merton (Harcourt Brace Jovanovich, 1948). This is one of the best-known books on a man's search for faith, written by a young man whose path led him first to baptism in the Catholic Church and ultimately to entry into a Trappist monastery.

Apologia Pro Vita Sua, by John Henry Newman (W. W. Norton, 1968). Once a well-known Anglican clergyman, Newman recanted his former criticism of the Roman Catholic Church and entered the priesthood in the 1840s. His conversion to Roman Catholicism rocked the Church of England and escalated the spread of anti-Catholicism in Victorian England. His autobiography, the title of which means "defense for my way of life," is an example of how wrestling with his beliefs changed one man's life forever.

The Essential Catholic Handbook: A Summary of Beliefs, Practices, and Prayers, by John O'Connor (Liguori Publications, 1997). This book covers fundamental Catholic doctrine, discusses the church's practices, outlines the liturgical seasons of the year, and defines the most important Catholic terms and topics.

Gift and Mystery: On the Fiftieth Anniversary of My Priestly Ordination, by Pope John Paul II (Image Books, 1999). In a personal, spiritual testimony, Pope John Paul II, the current head of the Catholic Church, describes his journey to the priesthood, discussing his childhood, education, the years of Nazi occupation in Europe that led him to dedicate his life to God, and his ministry within the Catholic Church.

Generous Lives: American Catholic Women Today, by Jane Redmont (Triumph Books, 1993). The issue of the role of women in the Catholic Church is one that generates a lot of interest. This book, based on personal interviews with more than one hundred Catholic women, aged seventeen to ninety, shows how different women see their lives in the church.

Sister Frances Carr

Eldress, Sabbathday Lake Shaker Community

"The most rewarding part of being a Shaker is knowing that over the years I have been able to return to God, through human beings, some of the wonderful benefits I have received from Father-Mother God by being placed with the Shakers."

The United Society of Believers, more commonly known as Shakers, was founded in 1747 in Manchester, England. They were called Shakers by their detractors because of their ecstatic and sometimes violent movements during worship. One member of this group was a young woman named Ann Lee (1736–1784), an outspoken figure who, among other things, championed the rights of women. In 1770, while imprisoned for publicly expressing her religious views, she experienced a series of visions. From that point on Ann Lee was acknowledged as the leader of the Shakers and known as Mother Ann.

In 1774 Mother Ann and eight of her followers boarded a run-down ship and set sail for America, landing in New York City after a perilous journey. She and her believers established the first Shaker community in the United States in 1776 and soon found themselves the center of attention because of their unusual beliefs and their very unpopular commitment to pacifism during the Revolutionary War. This new awareness brought not only converts, but persecution as well. The Shakers were harassed, beaten, stoned, driven out of towns, and imprisoned, all for religious reasons.

The Shakers share much in common with other Christian groups, but they are also unique. Among their defining characteristics are a belief in God as having both male and female aspects (the Father-Mother God), their belief that Jesus Christ (whom they call "the Christ") was a man and not the Son of God, their dedication to celibacy, their use of old-fashioned language such as "yea" and "nay" instead of "yes" and "no," their commitment to living in communities apart from the everyday world, and their strong work ethic.

Because they do not marry or have children, the Shakers must rely on converts in order to keep their faith going. At the height of their popularity, the Shakers had some five thousand members. Currently there are seven Shakers living in the last remaining

Shaker community of Sabbathday Lake in Maine. The Sabbathday Lake community was founded in 1783 by a group of Shaker missionaries. In less than a year's time nearly two hundred people had come to live there. On April 19, 1794, those residing there made an oral covenant with one another to consecrate their lives to God and formally create a community. Always referred to as "the least of Mother's children in the East," Sabbathday Lake was one of the numerically smallest and poorest of the eastern Shaker communities. But despite many difficulties, it endured, and today it is the only remaining active Shaker community.

Sister Frances Carr is the eldress of the Sabbathday Lake community, where she has lived since childhood.

When did you come to the Shakers?

In 1937, when I was ten years old. We had lost my father when I was just about two years old, and my mother had become, over the years, increasingly ill. She knew that she was not going to be able to take care of us much longer. I already had an older sister and brother living here at the Sabbathday Lake community, and I guess my mother believed that if she just held on, things would get better and we could all be together again. But things did not get better. They got progressively worse. Finally, she prepared my younger sister and me to come to the Shakers.

Sister Frances Carr   23

Were there a lot of children living at Sabbathday Lake?

When I came here, there were twelve little girls, aged five to fourteen, living in what was called the children's house. Many of these children would leave the Shakers within a year or two for various reasons. They were there because their parents were having marital difficulties or financial difficulties, and when things got straightened out, the parents would take their children back. For my sister and myself there was no place for us to go back to. My mother died soon after we arrived, and so we became charges of the Shaker community, with the understanding that when we came of age, we would make the decision either to leave the community or to remain here.

Was it common for the Shakers to take in children?

Oh, yea. I came to them at a time when the Shakers were still very actively involved in works of charity, which they had been involved in for many, many years. Their primary work was taking in children from broken homes, orphans, and so forth. I have always, since I became able to understand the situation, been so impressed by the fact that the community here at Sabbathday Lake had suffered great financial loss during the Great Depression, and yet they never turned away a needy child, even when things were very difficult. I think that is so wonderful.

What was your impression of the Shakers when you came to live with them?

In spite of the fact that my older brother and sister were living in the community, I never really had many occasions to visit them. We didn't have a car, and in those days if you didn't have a car, you didn't travel. Still, I guess I thought about them in a good sense. There was one difficulty that arose for me personally, which was that my mother had been a Catholic and my father was Baptist. After my father's death my mother reverted back to Catholicism, and a few years before I came to Sabbathday Lake I made my first Communion in the Catholic Church. I was very happy and interested in the Catholic Church. I was a regular communicant, and I knew that I would be giving that up by going to the Shakers. That was something of a hurdle for me.

What was your concept of God at the time you went to the Shakers?

I have always, from the time I could first understand the concept, believed in a God. I was trained to have daily prayers, and even though we lived in the world, my mother always maintained a rather strict Sabbath.

The Shakers see God as both Mother and Father. Did you have any trouble accepting that concept after your experience in the Catholic and Baptist Churches, where God is very much seen as male?

Sister Frances Carr   25

It did not occur to me at the time to get into the whole concept of our Mother-Father God. I didn't really think about it until I was in my teens. But I had other difficulties. I have to tell you that I was not an easy child for the Shakers to take care of. I had come to them expecting that I would be taken care of by a woman named Sister Jenny, a woman I had met and liked on the few occasions when I had visited the Shakers. But she occupied a position that did not involve taking care of children. On my first night, when I was introduced to Sister Mary, who would be our caretaker, I was disappointed and did not want to go with her. During the period when my mother was not very well, I had done a lot of caring for my younger sister, who was two years younger than I. To turn her over to another person was not easy. It made me quite defiant. I never did like Sister Mary. I do feel a little vindicated in the fact that she did later leave the community, so I don't think it was all my disposition that was at fault. She wasn't suited to community life, and I happened to be one of the targets of that for about two years. So that was hard for me.

I'm glad you told that story, because I think people often have the idea that life in a community like the Shakers' is idealized in some way.

Nay, life in a community is never perfect.

Why is it important to Shakers to leave behind the biological family to form a new family of believers?

The Shakers have based their lives on the life of Jesus. Jesus gave up his natural family. He and his disciples lived together communally, sharing all things in common. The Shakers do so as well. Jesus did not marry. The Shakers do not marry. Our whole way of living is based on the life of the Christ.

By doing that it seems your day-to-day life becomes your spirituality. Do you see Shakerism as less a religion than a lifestyle?

Well, it is a religious community. We are known as a Protestant monastic community, although we do not live in an enclosure like a monastery and we arc not as strictly separated from the world as many enclosed communities are. But religion is a daily part of our life, so yea, I would say it is a religion.

Yet the Shakers do not spend a great deal of time arguing dogma and theology, is that correct?

Oh, nay, we have no dogma. We feel that while we certainly look forward to eternity, and to a heavenly home, we also feel that every day that we live here we should build it up as a heaven on Earth. So while we do look forward to a future with God, we still have to do what God expects us to do in order to build up that heaven right now. Three times a day we meet for prayer, and prayer, religion, and work all seem to go hand in hand in our life.

In many Protestant religions the emphasis is almost wholly on the death of Christ being a way to achieve salvation. How do Shakers see Christ?

We believe that Jesus the man became "Christed" when he came out of his baptism with John and the voice from heaven said, "This is my beloved son." I have no problem with people of other faiths who do believe that Jesus died on the cross so that they could all be saved. It was a supreme sacrifice indeed. But we feel that each individual must work out his or her own salvation. I could never say, "I am saved and I am going to heaven because Jesus paid the price for me." Each of us has to find our own way to salvation.

And how do you do that?

By accepting that Christ spirit. Mother Ann, our founder, always referred to the Christ as making it possible for her to be who and what she was. It's a life-time work. I don't think any of us are going to reach perfection while we're here on Earth. It's a continual working, a continual laboring, for that perfection, which hopefully keeps us in the Christ spirit and close to our Father-Mother God.

What is the Shaker belief about life after death?

We feel that we do go to be with God. There is some similarity to the Catholic faith in that we believe that if we have not been living up to the Christ life while here on Earth, we are probably not going to go straight to heaven. Mother Ann talks, just as Jesus did, about laboring with people who are still working out their soul salvation in the land of the spirits. And every morning in our daily prayers, when we pray for the faithful departed, we also pray for those who are still working out their soul salvation, so that they may attain that higher heaven.

Is there a concept of hell in Shaker belief?

We don't believe in a raging fire or anything. I think that hell is our own conscience, those things that we do that take away our peace and torment us.

Is there any room for reincarnation in Shaker belief?

I don't think Shakers have ever believed in reincarnation. Although there are many people who visit our community who say that when they come back in the next life, they want to come back as a Shaker dog!

We do believe very strongly in what we call the communion of saints. When we lose loved ones, it's a terrible loss, of course. But we personally feel that their spirit hovers around us to help us in times of need. I have, over the last ten or twelve years, lost two or three people who were very, very special to me. One of them was Sister Mildred, who was my spiritual mother from the time that I was twelve. While the physical loss is very difficult to accept, I feel her spirit near me whenever I need it. I find myself talking to her if I'm in trouble. So we do very much believe in the communion of saints.

Do you see the Mother-Father God as a vengeful figure, as is so prevalent in some Christian traditions?

Nay, nay. Let's remember one thing: Why do we believe in a Father-Mother figure? Because if God is powerful and has the strength of a father, shouldn't there be a feminine nature as well with a gentleness to it? It's amazing to us to read in our church newspapers that so many churches are exploring the motherhood of God and it seems to be such a hurdle for them. It's such a natural way of looking at things for those of us who have been doing it for a long time.

I think that we hurt our Father-Mother. I think we disappoint them when we do wrong. But when I speak to young people who want to understand this concept, I say, "Your father and mother might be very disappointed in you when you do something wrong. But they still love you, and so they want to forgive you." Well, it's the same way with our Father-Mother God. We disappoint them. We hurt them if we do wrong and break their commandments. But they certainly are full of forgiveness and are willing to forgive us because their love is so vast.

You speak of the Father-Mother God as "them." Do you see them as two distinct entities?

We see them as one spirit with two natures.

Do Shakers believe that one can become the Christ, or simply a Christlike figure?

We are all able to have the Christ spirit. This is one of the greatest mistakes people make in the world today when trying to understand Shakerism. We have to go back to the very beginnings, when Mother Ann began working. The world was in a terrible state. People everywhere were looking for a messiah. I think for those poor, unenlightened people who were drawn to the charismatic, spiritual personality of Mother Ann, they could say that they thought they had found the second Christ. But always in her own words and her own testimonies, Mother Ann made it very clear that she was *not* the

Sister Frances Carr 31

Christ. She said it was the Christ spirit within her that allowed her to do the work that she did. She gave every bit of credit to the Christ, and not to herself. We do not feel that Mother Ann is the second coming of the Christ. We probably think of Mother Ann in the way that the Benedictines look upon Saint Benedict, or the Franciscans see Saint Francis. She is a revered, spiritual person, but not the Christ.

It has been suggested that Mother Ann based some of the foundations of Shakerism—such as the vow of celibacy—on the fact that she herself was terribly afraid of sex and men, and not on any actual religious conviction. Do you think this in any way negates what she taught?

She certainly had trouble with her husband. But remember, Mother Ann first became viewed as out of the ordinary when she challenged the Episcopal Church in England and their policy of catering to those people who could give them money. The poor people were left out, and that riled her up. She protested against it to the point where she was thrown in prison. A lot of people today who write about Shakers say that Mother Ann may have become so psychologically disturbed by the death of her four children that this is what made her embrace celibacy. But from the time she was a teenager she fought against marriage. In those days a young girl was forced to be married. She did not want to be married. She felt that if she lived the life of the Christ, she had to be celibate, as he was.

But isn't a spirituality that might be based in part on what could have been psychological neurosis one that is open to question?

I think that everything Mother Ann did, she did from a very, very strong faith. Her faith is what motivated her teachings. I can't think of anything she did that might be a negation.

Well, celibacy, for example. If she advocated celibacy because she was afraid of marriage, is that really a valid point of her faith?

I think she did indeed have a very, very unhappy marriage. But even before she got married, she was preaching celibacy. She was forced into marriage like many women were. When I try to explain to people why we don't marry, I explain that Jesus didn't marry, and because our life is patterned after his, we don't marry. Secondly, in a religious community—and the Shaker community is a very different community compared to most religious communities—we have brothers and sisters all living in the same community. If I were married, I would want my husband to have the best position in the community. I would want my children to be very special. And that's not possible in a Shaker community, where we need to think of the good of the community as a whole. But the underlying emphasis on why we are celibate is that we follow the life of the Christ. And also because we believe that sexuality is one of the things that can draw us away from God. I don't mean that to sound puritanical, because certainly there's nothing at all wrong with sexuality. We recognize that marriage is a sacrament in most churches. But it's not for us.

Obviously, because of the vow of celibacy, Shakerism can only continue if new people come into the community. The number of Shakers is now very low. Do you worry about the community dying out?

Of course I do. We would be very naive indeed to say that we are not concerned. We pray constantly about it. We pray every day that more people will be drawn into the Shaker way. I find it rather encouraging to know that when Mother Ann first came to America, there were eight Shakers. If we can get our eighth one back, the community will be at that same population. There is a tremendous interest in us on the part of the outside world today, and hopefully, if it's God's will, some of these people will become Shakers.

What would attract someone in modern times to come into Shakerism?

You know, we sit and talk about that sometimes. We see the unhappiness of people in the world and we wonder, "Why don't they want to be here at the Shaker village?" We have a wonderful life. Those of us who serve as elders and trustees of course have responsibilities, and the other members do too. But we are free from so many of the cares of the world that people have to deal with. We're free to be ourselves. We are constantly surrounded by members of the Christ family. If we need time alone, we certainly have that, but we are never lonely. So we don't understand why people wouldn't want this. Why wouldn't people want to come where they are free to worship, where they are free to be themselves, where we wear no masks, and where life is good. I don't understand it. We do continue, all of the time, to receive letters from people inquiring about joining the community. But there is always something that prevents them from being able to give up their life and come here.

What kinds of things?

Everyone assumes it's celibacy, but celibacy does not seem to be the stumbling block. What causes the most problems is the idea of giving up one's independence. Of course, we do have some restrictions on membership. We have decided that we will not take anyone over the age of fifty-five because, quite frankly, we do not want to turn the community into a nursing home. We can't take anyone who is still in any kind of legal debt. There are many restrictions that have kept a lot of older people from coming. But we do get new members. Our youngest member, who is in the novitiate period, has only been here for a few months.

I find it interesting that you talk about giving up worldly cares when one comes to the Shakers, because to an outsider it might seem that your life, especially the very hard physical work that you do on a daily basis, is much harder than anything in the outside world.

That's a good point. A lot of people idealize Shakerism as an easy life. And it's not an easy life at all. It's a hard life. We work very hard. Our official motto is "Hands to work and hearts to God," and we put that into effect every single day. To the Shaker, the relationship between work and religion is inseparable. There is work in religion and religion in work, and the two go hand in hand. No one at the Shaker village ever retires. From the very beginning the Shakers believed that even the spiritual heads of the communities had to do something with their hands, had to work to help the community. Today I serve as trustee and eldress alongside Brother Arnold, who is the male elder. And I also work in the kitchen every day. That's my work. I prepare meals every single day. Everybody has to work, and it's a good thing.

Do you resent all the interest in Shaker life on the part of the outside world, who might ignore the religious aspects of Shakerism and see you as an oddity or a curiosity?

I am not one of those who do. Sometimes some of the younger brothers, who are more often outside working where the public sees them, are asked if they can be photographed. I think they resent it more than I do. I always say that if it were not for the museum we run, some of our dearest friends would never know us. I do think there is too much emphasis on the furniture, but if it's a way of drawing people more closely to the life, then I guess I can live with it.

It strikes me as ironic that a faith some people look upon as being so old-fashioned was one of the faiths that was first physically attacked and ridiculed for holding progressive views long before they were popular.

Yea. And even now people still come here and are somewhat disappointed to see that we have electric lights and telephones, televisions, and computers. We are very, very concerned with the social issues of the day. For many years Shakers did not vote. Mother Ann always believed that, if we got into that, it would cause divisions within the community. But we did begin voting in the 1960s because we became very concerned about social issues of the day. For example, we were concerned about the poor, and that's when we began cooking and serving meals at a homeless shelter here in Maine. We became very concerned about children's rights. People used to say to us, and we used to say to one another, "Well, if you don't vote, then you can't complain." So we began voting.

What was it that made you decide to stay with the Shakers all those years ago?

Well, I was probably the least likely candidate to those who knew me. When I was a little girl, I used to think of being a nun, because I was a Catholic child. I was always drawn to Mary. I came here with that same feeling. I was very drawn to some of the older sisters, who seemed to have a wonderful sense of spirituality, but for the first few years I did not give staying a great deal of thought. When I left the children's house and moved into the main house, I found a wonderful spiritual mother in Sister Mildred, and I began to see things very differently. She was very spiritual, but she never pushed Shaker theology onto the young people in their care.

There were eight of us, eight teenagers, and one by one I saw most of these people leave the community, including my younger sister. I guess my first feelings were feelings of pity. I saw how hurtful it was to the Shakers when people left, even though they knew that the children were not there by choice and had the freedom to leave when they were old enough. But I saw that they were still hurt. I think I decided that I should do something to change that situation.

Well, pity is not a good basis for choosing a religious life, and Sister Mildred realized that. But I think she also saw that there was some possibility in my truly becoming interested in being a Shaker. We had many long talks about it. She made me very aware of what I would be giving up to be a Shaker, but also what I would be gaining. By the time I was twenty, I had really become convinced that I wanted to remain. I signed the church covenant when I was twenty-one, and though there have been difficult times in my life, I can say in complete honesty that I have never regretted the choice that I made.

Can you even imagine what other kind of life you might have had?

I see some of my girlhood friends. We've kept in touch. I picture myself sometimes in their shoes, and it's not what I would want. My sister married and had six children. She wanted a family life. I am now blessed with many nieces and nephews with whom I have a wonderful relationship. But that life was not for me.

What has been, for you, the most rewarding part of your time spent in the Shaker faith?

The most rewarding part of being a Shaker is knowing that over the years I have been able to return to God, through human beings, some of the wonderful benefits I have received from Father-Mother God by being placed with the Shakers. I think that I am grateful that even though I had a very difficult time growing up here, it made me a stronger woman. It made me more aware of what other people go through. I am grateful that I am continuing to live in a place where, hopefully, we can be a little beacon of light to the world and show people that it is possible to give up worldly possessions and put the material things second to the spiritual, where we can welcome and help anyone who needs that help.

What would your advice be to young people trying to find their own spiritual path?

Not to give up. To turn in prayer to whatever power they look upon as being the God, the spiritual power. To go to that power for help often. To stand firm among their peers and not be turned away from the good just to be popular. But mostly to turn to prayer. That has helped me all through my life. When I was a young girl, I used to continually lose socks while doing the wash, which was one of my chores. I always had one missing, and the sister who took care of me finally lost patience and told me that if it happened again, I would not be able to go to the movies, which we had here every Thursday night. Well, I did. I lost a sock. And I didn't want to miss the movie. So as a very little child I prayed that I would find that sock. And I found it way down in the bottom of a tub. Ever since then I have believed in the power of prayer. In happy times we should pray. In difficult times we should pray earnestly. No matter what your religion is, there is a higher power that you can seek help from.

FOR MORE INFORMATION

ON-LINE RESOURCES

Sabbathday Lake Shaker Village
www.shaker.lib.me.us

This is the official Web site of the Sabbathday Lake Shaker Community. It contains information about the Shaker Museum, events being held at Sabbathday Lake, and Shakerism in general.

BOOKS

The Sabbathday Lake Shakers: An Introduction to the Shaker Heritage, by Sister R. Mildred Barker (The Shaker Press, 1985). Written by a member of the Sabbathday Lake community—and Sister Carr's spiritual mentor—this book provides a history of that community and an introduction to Shaker beliefs.

Mother Ann Lee: Morning Star of the Shakers, by Nardi Reeder Campion (University Press of New England, 1990). A biography of the controversial founder of the Shaker faith.

Growing Up Shaker, by Sister Frances A. Carr (The United Society of Shakers, 1994). The life story of Sister Frances A. Carr, the eldress of the Sabbathday Lake community.

The Shaker World: Art, Life, Belief, by John T. Kirk (Harry N. Abrams, 1997). Documents, diaries, letters, and photographs show the evolution of Shaker religious beliefs and practices, and the art and furniture produced by Shaker craftspeople.

God Among the Shakers: A Search for Stillness and Faith at Sabbathday Lake, by Suzanne Skees (Hyperion, 1998). The story of a writer who lived for a time with the Shaker community at Sabbathday Lake and discovered many insights into their history and their beliefs.

Simple Gifts: A Memoir of a Shaker Village, by June Sprigg (Knopf, 1998). Sprigg spent one summer as a teenager working as a tour guide at Canterbury Shaker Village in New Hampshire. In this memoir she discusses her relationship with the seven women who made up the community (now defunct) and how living among the community affected her life. In an interesting historical note she examines the infamous split between the community of Canterbury and the community at Sabbathday Lake over their visions of the future of Shaker life.

The Shaker Experience in America: A History of the United Society of Believers, by Stephen J. Stein (Yale University Press, 1994). Although this book, which draws on written and oral testimony by Shakers over the past two centuries, is definitely scholarly in nature, it can be read by anyone who wants a thorough history of the Shaker communities in America.

Rabbi Sheldon Zimmerman

President, Hebrew Union College—
Jewish Institute of Religion

"I've always felt personally motivated by the messianic hope, in this sense—that there can be a better tomorrow. That sense that the future can be better, and that I can work to help make it better, has always been a powerful part of who I am."

The origins of Judaism, one of the oldest of the world's religions, are traced to around the time of 1800 B.C.E., when Jews believe that God made a covenant with the patriarch Abraham, who lived in what is now present-day Iraq, to form a nation that would worship him as the one true God. Though there is no reason given in the Hebrew Scriptures for why Abraham was chosen specifically, Jewish tradition states that it was because he rejected his people's practice of worshiping many gods (his father is believed to have owned a shop that sold idols), and instead believed in only one supreme God. It

44

is from Abraham, his son Isaac, and his grandson Jacob (also called Israel, the name of the modern Jewish state) that the Jewish people trace their history.

Originally organized into twelve different tribes descended from the sons of Abraham's grandson Jacob, the Jewish people were united into one kingdom under the leadership of Saul around 1050 B.C.E. Their second king, David, established Jerusalem as the religious and political center of Jewish life, and the First Temple was built there by the third king, Solomon. After the death of Solomon, Judaism went through a long period of internal conflicts and conquest by other cultures. When a series of revolts led to the destruction of Jerusalem and its Temple in 70 C.E., the Jews were scattered throughout the known world and were prohibited from setting foot in Jerusalem. Because of this, local synagogues became the new center of Jewish life, and authority shifted from one primary leader to local scholars and teachers, or rabbis.

Throughout history the Jewish people have frequently found themselves the target of oppression. The most horrific period of persecution came in the 1930s and 1940s, when Adolph Hitler and the German Nazi Party carried out the Holocaust, the attempted extermination of all Jews in Europe. About six million people were killed in one of the world's most chilling examples of religious and racial intolerance.

Jewish faith is based on the belief that there is one

God and that he is the creator of all that exists. Jews believe that they are able to purify their lives and draw closer to God by fulfilling his commandments, but unlike Christianity, the tradition does not believe that Jesus Christ was a savior sent to rescue humankind from sin. The most sacred texts of Judaism are the Torah, which contains Holy Scripture revealed to the Jewish leader Moses by God on Mount Sinai and other holy writings, and the Talmud, a collection of stories, laws, debates about moral choices, and other writings pertaining to the faith.

There are currently about eighteen million Jews throughout the world and three main forms of Judaism. Orthodox Judaism is the oldest and most traditional form of Judaism. Orthodox Jews observe the religion as closely to its original form as possible and see every word in their sacred texts as being divinely inspired. Reform Judaism is a liberal form followed by about 70 percent of the Jews in the world. Its adherents observe the ethical laws of Judaism but leave up to the individual the decision whether to follow or ignore other traditional laws. Conservative Judaism is a mainline movement midway between Reform and Orthodox.

Rabbi Sheldon Zimmerman is the president of Hebrew Union College–Jewish Institute of Religion, the largest educational institution in the Reform movement. A rabbi since 1970, he has served as both a spiritual and an academic leader.

What was your relationship to your spirituality when you were a teenager?

It was a very different world then from what it is today. I'm fifty-six now, so this was quite some time ago. I grew up in Toronto, and I am an eleventh-generation rabbi, possibly even fifteenth or sixteenth generation. I grew up in a home that was very traditional and traditionally observant. At the same time, we were trying to find our way in the New World, so to speak. Most of my family were immigrants. Therefore, my spirituality was connected both with acknowledging where I was coming from as a human being in terms of years and years of tradition, as well as with being a child of a new and modern world.

Did you enjoy attending religious services?

My paternal grandfather was a rabbi in downtown Toronto. My maternal grandparents were members of a different congregation. I would go back and forth between the two. But when I was nine, we moved to another area of the city. Rather than continue going with one grandparent or another, at that time we found another synagogue, which was a really interesting blend of tradition and modernity. There I could fully practice what was important to me, which was the ritual and symbols of my faith, but at the same time I could be modern.

Rabbi Sheldon Zimmerman

What did you love about the rituals?

My home was embraced by ritual. You can imagine, say if you're Protestant, having in your family generations of ministers going far back into your history, or if you're Catholic, having an uncle or brother in every generation who was a priest. That's what my family had, generations of men who had been rabbis. These were deeply devout families. The observance of the Sabbath and of festivals was really the rhythm of our lives. This is very different from how it is in families that are transient or separated or fragmented. Today extended families are nonexistent for many people. But we had that. The Sabbath was spent with grandparents. The festivals were spent with grandparents. The seder observance was with grandparents. So my life was filled with these traditions. Now, I don't want to give the impression that this was an ultratraditional, ghettoized Jewish family. It was not. I lived in a wider world. I watched hockey. I played football. It wasn't as if this was a life apart or a life separate from the rest of the world.

You grew up during the years of World War II, when the Holocaust claimed many Jewish people in Europe. Did that affect your family at all?

I remember, as a young person, being totally embraced by observance and festival and the joy of being Jewish and the wonder of it all. At the same time, the stories of the

Paths of Faith

Holocaust were just coming through. We had one rela-
tive who came out of the Holocaust, a cousin, and I
remember he had deep eyes that were so profoundly sad.
He had been in the camps. It was hard to talk with him.
We talked a little bit, but there was a strangeness about
him that frightened me, and there was something of a
desire on my part not to hear about great-grandparents
having been killed in the Holocaust or about great-uncles
and -aunts being destroyed. Many people in the family
died. That was a reality. It's hard to remember when it was
talked about, but I remember that it was.

How did news of the Holocaust make you feel about being Jewish?

There was, in the 1940s and 1950s, a lot of anti-
Semitism in the world, and I felt that. Today it's almost
minimal compared with what we had then. There was a
sense of insecurity, and we often felt that we had to
watch our backs. We did grow up with that. But
nonetheless, there was simply a joy about being Jewish
that was stronger than any of that.

*Do you remember anything in particular about Jewish spirituality
that really moved you as a young adult?*

I always loved to study, but the thing I loved the
most was the music. My father had a wonderful voice,
and he used to sing in a choir. I have a picture of myself

Rabbi Sheldon Zimmerman   49

at about the age of seven surrounded by my grandfather and his sons, including my father, all garbed in choir dress. They used to sing together, and I loved hearing it. I loved the observance of the Sabbath with the singing of melodies. I loved the observance of all the holidays. There wasn't one without singing. As a boy I could sit and listen to great music, to cantors chanting, all of that stuff, forever. And I still could. The music was part of me, and is still very much part of the fabric of my life.

The greatest sense of loss for me is that I was never really able to sing for my grandfather the way he could sing for me. You know how sometimes you hear melodies in your head, but the music that comes out of you when you try to sing them is only a faint shadow of what you hear? That's how I feel about my singing. I have almost perfect pitch, but what comes out isn't a great voice. I sometimes think I would trade all of my capacity to preach and teach and write and speak to be able to sound great singing.

As far as the rest of it goes, Jewish spirituality was simply the calendar of my life. Again, the secular holidays were there as well, but the real cycle of my life revolved around the Jewish holy days. Sabbath was Sabbath, and that was a day filled with a certain routine. It was a wonderful day of renewal and discovery and prayer. So there was the connection to music and to study and to prayer, and a great connection to family that ran through all of that.

Some people from immigrant families say they sometimes felt a need to escape their traditions. Did you ever feel that?

In my life I very much felt the need to be a good citizen, to be modern. I did look for ways to get away from some of the immigrant stuff that made me feel insecure. Although my father was an immigrant and my mother's family were immigrants, I clearly wanted to be a member of the community and culture of Canada and North America. There was a sense that there was a world somewhat separate from the world my family came from. But I also cherished what they came from, so I tried to combine the two by finding my own synagogue, one that spoke to both of my lives. I went to a place where there was dignity and decorum. The rabbi preached in impeccable English. There was a sense of community activism and social justice. At the same time, there were also the traditions and music that I loved. It was a great combination.

Did you ever feel that your Jewishness or your family's Jewish heritage was holding you back in any way from being the modern person you wanted to be?

It was more the immigrant thing than it was the Jewish thing. I think I tried more to distance myself from the immigrant experience, which, in my mind, continued to maintain the old country traditions in the

Rabbi Sheldon Zimmerman

face of a changing world. That's where the struggle was. For example, I sometimes felt a sense of embarrassment when my grandparents insisted on doing things the old way or when they didn't speak English quite right. It was more that than a religious issue. But I think that struggle still continues in me, a struggle between the part of me that adores tradition and the part of me that embraces modernity. It's an ongoing issue.

Where was God in all of this for you?

God was and is everywhere, in personal prayer at night and in the morning. My relationship to God has evolved through the years, and a number of things have moved me. One is a sense of gratitude for life. I don't have to be alive. I really sensed, even as a kid, that every day was a gift. Each day was a precious empty vessel waiting to be filled in some kind of way. It's hard for me to sit still, not because I'm hyperactive, but because things are waiting to be done. I've always had something of a sense of urgency to be cocreative with God. Now, that's my adult self looking back and trying to describe how I felt. But I always had a very traditional sense of gratitude for life and for another day.

That was one part of my relationship to God. The other part was that God was calling me to make a difference somehow. I felt that I had to do something with my life to make a difference in the world. Eventually that led me to go into the rabbinate instead of going where I was heading, which was toward a doctorate in philosophy.

Why did you change your plans?

I was finishing up my master's degree when I had a fellowship in philosophy offered to me by a university. I really struggled with the decision of what to do. I was a kid who had been very active in youth group. Growing up, I was involved in youth group and with my congregation. I was always pushing to be a leader in those groups. I came out of that background and didn't know what to do next. So when I was offered this fellowship, I had to decide what I was going to do with my life that would make a difference. I wanted to find a way to take my life and consecrate it in a unique way to serve the Jewish people, with whom I did and do feel intimately connected.

And you chose to become a rabbi?

I did. I chose to go to rabbinical school. But I chose to do it within the Reform movement, not the traditional background I came from. It was almost as if becoming a Reformed Jew was my way of blending the modern with the traditional.

How did your choice of studying within the Reform movement go over with your family?

Rabbi Sheldon Zimmerman   53

Are you kidding? My father, bless his memory, said that my grandfather was turning over in his grave when I first started studying. That was at the beginning. He later made peace with it, after he met some of my professors and was taken with their knowledge and their piety. Though it was not his way, he nonetheless accepted it. But at the beginning it was very, very difficult.

Why did you think becoming a rabbi should be the next step in your spiritual path?

I remember at one point reading Martin Buber's book *I and Thou* and really spending time with it. It made me recognize that what I considered a philosophical, almost objective stance to spirituality was not really possible. Just looking at texts and traditions from the outside wasn't adequate. I knew I had to take a very personal, existential stance to my spirituality with regard to my relationship to God and my covenant with other people. That's when I really shifted my focus from purely academic concerns to more personal ones. Even at that point I had been considering remaining in academia as a professor. But then I decided that I had to go out and serve. I decided to go out and serve and take a stance. I've always believed that life is a gift and the need to serve is a gift. That personal relationship I had with God, even in my youth, convinced me of that.

Paths of Faith

There is a history in Judaism of believers being able to argue with God. Do you think that's what you were doing, in a sense, by choosing the Reform movement over the Orthodox?

I was arguing with my own faith. I was arguing with God. I came into a movement that wasn't mine. Many of my colleagues grew up in the Reform movement, but I didn't. It was a different world for me.

How does the Reform movement differ from the one you were raised in?

The Reform movement takes change very seriously. It accepts Judaism as having been a changing religion. Secondly, Reform takes personal accountability and personal choice very seriously. We believe that not everything is black and white. Not everything is God-given or God-determined. We believe that you have to find within your religious faith that which speaks to you most eloquently, persuasively, and compellingly. That conjoining of change and modernity on one hand with a sense of personal choice on the other is what I think really distinguishes the movement.

Now, it also means that we don't accept everything as literal revelation from God either. We believe that the Bible is the product of our people's attempt to try and understand God's will in their lives over the years, where the Orthodox tradition teaches that it is all God-given.

Rabbi Sheldon Zimmerman

We take individual choice and the reality of change very seriously. Our challenge, and the danger in Reform, is that freedom can become license. Some people exercise personal choice as convenience and don't take seriously the voice of God. So really the challenge of Reform for me, and especially for our young people, is how we find distinctive meaning in our life.

Do you think spirituality should always be a driving force behind what we do with our lives?

This is something that always motivated me as a young man. It was making a difference, serving a higher purpose, and knowing that my life could have meaning in service to others. That was always clearly there. That didn't mean that I wasn't self-centered or doing my own thing as a teenager. That was clearly there too. But I knew that it wasn't going to be my whole life. And I think that's the challenge for today's young people. If you talk to people about me, they will tell you about the struggle I went through to decide how to live my life. There was one group that thought, "Of course he's going to be a rabbi." There was another group that thought, "What do you mean *he's* going to be a rabbi?" Because there were moments when I truly challenged everything I was taught.

But don't you think that willingness to challenge things makes you stronger?

Absolutely. They often say that the best students at our college are the ones who were rebellious as teenagers. Often you take the worst students from religious school and they become the best rabbis. Some of the most healing people in this world are the ones who are the most cynical or questioning, because they have a desire to fight the things they find troubling.

Do you ever get tired of the fight?

There are days when I want a rest. But you go on. That's probably what led me to come back into academia. I was a rabbi in New York from 1970 to 1985 at a major congregation in midtown Manhattan. From 1985 to 1996 I was a rabbi at a temple in Dallas, which was probably the third-largest congregation in the United States. And it was a wonderful life. But it was also tiring, and I needed a rest.

How difficult was it taking what had for most of your life been a personal spirituality and suddenly being a rabbi in charge of a congregation where your spirituality was out there for everyone to see?

It was difficult in this sense: It was difficult because you always had to be on. The challenge was trying to find spiritual time for yourself. I had to learn how to pray while I was leading prayer, and not become so self-involved with things like worrying about how my voice sounded or if I was making my point.

Rabbi Sheldon Zimmerman

How did you do that?

It was a challenge. First, I worked to keep prayerfulness as a part of my life. That was not easy to do. The second thing was easy, and that was that I found tremendous fulfillment in service to others and in helping others to find their way. Sometimes you don't even know when you touch others. You may not know until much later, or maybe never at all. Sometimes people will come up to me and say, "Do you remember when you said this or that?" And sometimes I don't even remember saying it. I don't remember even the meaning of it. But it was something that made a difference to someone.

In a sense, everything I did as a rabbi, whether it was sitting with little kids or being at a youth retreat or teaching a class or leading a funeral, was more fulfilling and more rewarding than anything I can think of doing. Now, as I said, the problem is finding yourself drained of your own spirituality. It's like being a mother. Mothers who give birth to infants have an instinctual need to feed them. But unless they take care of themselves, and take their own strength from something, they'll have nothing left to give. One of the great challenges of being a rabbi is continuing to learn and to grow spiritually, and to observe in such a way that you have something to give to others.

Have there been moments of doubt for you over the years when you wondered if God was really there or if what you believe really made sense?

Not moments of doubt, but there have been moments of personal questioning. For example, perhaps when dealing with the death or the sickness of a young person, I might think the situation is very unfair. I remember once I had to officiate at a funeral where a very young mother and child had died together in a terrible fire. That was hard. I could give you instance after instance where something unfair happened. Those are moments of profound questioning. And then there are moments when you think people ought to go one way, but they either aren't ready or aren't willing to go that way. You spend all of your energy trying to show them the way to go, and then you come home completely depleted of energy. You come home to your wife and your kids, who have a claim on you as well, and you wonder why you're doing it all. There are profound moments of disappointment in all our lives, moments when promises are not kept or negotiations go wrong or when what you think should happen just doesn't happen. Sometimes things that you think are important, other people think are totally irrelevant. Those are hard times.

So how do you renew yourself at those times?

Prayer. Quietness. Study. And lots of hugs from little kids. I found my work with young people, and still find it, very rewarding and very renewing.

Rabbi Sheldon Zimmerman   59

Do you find that sometimes the joy of God is much more accessible for young people?

There's a tremendous joy in young people. As I mentioned, in my youth I found tremendous joy in music, in dance, and in tradition, and that remains a part of me. Give me a good recording of Jewish music and I'm reborn.

Do you think that sometimes arguing or debating theological points gets in the way of remembering the true meaning of spirituality?

Absolutely. Sometimes we need to do rituals just for the sake of enjoying them. We forget the higher calling. I always try to remind our students that the call at Sinai was for us to become a kingdom of priests and holy people. All the rest of it was just particulars. And you shouldn't confuse the particulars with the call. Sometimes I refer to this problem as the religious thermometer of our Jewishness, where someone will say, "Where I am is fine, and to my right they're crazy and to my left they're all Gentiles." That's the kind of thing that gets in the way.

Do you believe that someone born outside the tradition can become fully Jewish, or is it a faith you need to be born into and raised in?

Oh, yes, I think someone can become Jewish. I think it's hard, because if you haven't been raised in it, then

Paths of Faith

the folk component is missing as well as the religious component. But it can be done. It takes time. One can make the religious affirmations about the one God and the God of Covenant and the God of Sinai, and the hopes and dreams of a better future, in a shorter time. But the notion of becoming part of a people, part of a folk, takes much longer, especially when many of the people think that their ethnic peculiarity is what makes them truly Jewish.

Do you think people sometimes mistake Jewish cultural heritage for Jewish religion?

That's when you get, for example, Eastern European Jewish descendants insisting that latkes are the traditional Hanukkah dish, where Israelis, who come out of a different milieu, insist that jelly doughnuts are the traditional dish. Really it's anything fried in oil, but people bring their ethnic differences into it and insist that only their way is the right way. It's hard to become part of a people who say that being Jewish is a particular feeling you have, and may even think that it has nothing at all to do with their spirituality. Some see Jewishness simply as an inheritance and claim not to believe anything religious at all. That's problematic for converts because those arguments and fears about such things often get in the way of people wanting to become Jewish.

Rabbi Sheldon Zimmerman   61

The idea that you are a particular faith simply because your ances-tors were that faith is not uncommon in many religious traditions. Do you think it's legitimate?

It's like an old chair that you leave in the attic. You can't transmit your feelings about that old chair to any-one else. They have to experience it for themselves. It's the same with religion and with spirituality. You don't have feelings about it or experiences related to it simply because your ancestors did. You have to have your own relationship to it.

What, to you, is the ultimate goal of a life spent in the Jewish tradi-tion?

I've always felt personally motivated by the mes-sianic hope, in this sense—that there can be a better tomorrow. That sense that the future can be better, and that I can work to help make it better, has always been a powerful part of who I am.

Is there some final outcome you think about?

That someday there will be a day of peace and jus-tice. As we say when we end our prayer service, I hope for the day when God will be one and God's names will be one again. That's the prophetic promise.

Do you spend time thinking about when that will happen?

No, but I act as if it could happen tomorrow.

What advice do you have for young people who might be searching for a spiritual path?

Look hard. Know that searching is a wonderful thing. First of all, affirm the search. I think the search and the voyage are the point. We are all on a journey. And sometimes, like Moses wandering in the desert for forty years, we never get there. But we are on an extraordinary journey of redemption and hope. So take that journey very seriously. Look hard at the variety of religions and possibilities. Read a lot. Meet with people from different traditions. Celebrate the humanness that joins us all together, as well as those particularities that make up our differences. I think enjoying the journey is the most important part.

FOR MORE INFORMATION

ON-LINE RESOURCES

Shamash: The Jewish Internet Consortium
www.shamash.org

There are hundreds of sites related to Judaism on the Web, and Shamash lists almost all of them. It's a fantastic place to look for what's out there on one easy-to-use site.

Anti-Defamation League
www.adl.org

The ADL is one of the most active Jewish organizations in the world, and its site is a fantastic source of information about current events related to Judaism, including the work to stop hate groups targeting Jews and others, Holocaust studies, and the ongoing struggle for peace in the Middle East.

BOOKS

What Do Jews Believe? The Spiritual Dimensions of Judaism, by David Ariel (Schocken Books, 1995). An engaging exploration of the elements of Jewish belief, covering major ethical, ritual, and theological topics related to the different Jewish movements.

Embracing the Covenant: Converts to Judaism Talk about Why and How, by Allan L. Berkowitz and Patti Moskovitz (Jewish Lights Publications, 1996). These personal stories of more than fifty converts describe both the difficulties and the joys of converting to Judaism.

Choosing a Jewish Life: A Handbook for People Converting to Judaism and for Their Family and Friends, by Anita Diamant

(Schocken Books, 1997). A practical guide for anyone possibly interested in following the Jewish path.

Living Judaism: The Complete Guide to Jewish Belief, Tradition, and Practice, by Wayne D. Dosick (HarperSanFrancisco, 1998). An overview of Jewish philosophy and theology, rituals, and customs, this book is useful for both those already involved in Jewish life and those beginning to explore Judaism.

The How-to Handbook for Jewish Living, by Ronald H. Isaacs and Kerry M. Olitzky (K'tav Publishing House, 1993). A collection of information about what it means to live as a Jewish person today.

Basic Judaism, by Milton Steinberg (Harcourt Brace Jovanovich, 1986). This small volume is considered one of the best introductions to Judaism ever written, and explains both traditional and modern Judaism in a readable way that makes the concepts easy to understand.

Jewish Literacy: The Most Important Things You Need to Know About the Jewish Religion, Its People, and Its History, by Rabbi Joseph Telushkin (Morrow, 1991). Organized by subject, this reference book provides a wealth of information on virtually all aspects of the Jewish religion, from the very beginnings of Jewish history to modern-day issues.

Rabbi Sheldon Zimmerman

Karma Lekshe Tsomo

American Buddhist Nun and Cofounder, Sakyadhita: The International Association of Buddhist Women

"I knew very early on that this was my path. But there is quite a distance between recognizing your path and making a lifelong commitment to it."

With at least half a million practitioners worldwide, Buddhism is not only one of the great religions in Asia, but it is quickly gaining popularity in Western countries as well. Buddhism was founded in northern India by Siddhartha Gautama, a wealthy prince who lived from around 563 to 485 B.C. At the age of twenty-nine, he left his wife, child, and kingdom in order to seek the answers to life's questions. Though he initially explored the traditional teachings of Hinduism, he ultimately rejected those teachings and followed his own path. In 533 B.C., it is believed, he reached enlightenment and assumed the title of Buddha, which means "one who has awakened."

The Buddha encouraged following what he called the Middle Way, teaching that the road to Nirvana (enlightenment) came from walking a path between the practices of extreme asceticism and of overindulgence. While Buddhism has no single authoritative text, the teachings of the Buddha (called Buddhadharma) and commentaries on those teachings—called sutras, or discourses—have been compiled.

Buddhists do not see the Buddha as God, or as a god. He is believed to be a man who achieved enlightenment through study, meditation, and right livelihood, and Buddhists believe that all people can achieve the same enlightenment through the same practices. Buddhism does not teach the need for a personal savior. Instead, they believe in reincarnation, or rebirth, the concept that one must go through many cycles of birth, living, and death in various realms of existence, learning all that is necessary to attain enlightenment and reach Nirvana.

Just as there are many different forms of Christianity, there are different branches of Buddhism, which are geographically and philosophically distinct. Each tradition, in turn, has many schools. Theravada Buddhism is practiced mainly in Burma, Cambodia, Laos, Sri Lanka, Thailand, and parts of Vietnam. Mahayana Buddhism is the predominant religion in China, Japan, Korea, Vietnam, Mongolia, Tibet, and parts of Russia. While there are a number of recognized Buddhist figures—

Karma Lekshe Tsomo

particularly His Holiness the Dalai Lama of Tibet—each tradition of Buddhism has its own leaders, and there is no formal authority for Buddhism as a whole.

Karma Lekshe Tsomo is an American Buddhist nun who has been ordained in the Tibetan, Korean, and Chinese traditions of Buddhism. A writer, lecturer, and teacher, she is particularly interested in the role of women in Buddhism and is the cofounder of Sakyadhita: The International Association of Buddhist Women. *Sakyadhita* means "daughters of the Buddha," and the objectives of the organization are (1) to promote world peace through the practice of the Buddha's teachings, (2) to create a network of communication for Buddhist women throughout the world, (3) to promote harmony and understanding among the various Buddhist traditions, (4) to encourage and help educate women as teachers of Buddhadharma, (5) to provide improved facilities for women to study and practice the teachings, and (6) to help establish the bhikshuni sangha (community of fully ordained nuns) where it does not currently exist.

Were you raised in the Buddhist tradition?

I was raised Christian, in the Presbyterian Church. I was very spiritually inclined, and I enjoyed the atmosphere of the church and getting in touch with my own inner spiritual life. I also had a lot of questions about what we're all doing here and how to live a happier life.

Like many young people, I felt like I was under a lot of peer pressure and that many of the values of mainstream society were not ones I was comfortable with. So I was looking for alternatives to those values.

Did you find it in the Christian Church?

I liked going to church. At the same time, I was really examining the values presented in the Christian faith, which was the only thing available to me at that time, and was having difficulty finding people who actually lived up to those values. I looked at Christ's teachings on loving kindness, compassion, and concern for the down-trodden, and didn't find many people living up to those teachings. I also saw some hypocrisy, so I was looking for something different.

Were there particular questions you had about religious faith?

As a young person I had a lot of questions, especially about death. I wanted to know what happened to people after they died. I asked everyone I could find but didn't get a satisfactory answer to this question. I did a lot of philosophical questioning but didn't get clear answers from the people around me.

You didn't accept the Christian concept of going to heaven or hell after death?

Karma Lekshe Tsomo   69

No, that seemed a bit too simple. And that made things difficult for me. I respected the ethical framework of Christianity, as well as the teachings on compassion and the contemplative aspects. But for me to say that I believed in a creator God when in fact I did not would have been to lie. I felt that to actually uphold the moral principles of the Christian tradition I had to be honest about my beliefs, and I couldn't honestly believe in the notion of an external, wrathful, omnipotent creator God who demanded obedience or would send a person to hell.

How did you happen to discover Buddhism?

By coincidence, my family name was Zenn. Because I had that name, I started reading about Zen Buddhism when I was quite young. My mother says that I announced I was a Buddhist at the age of eleven. I remember reading my first book on Buddhism and really resonating with it, thinking, "This is it!"

What did you find in Buddhism that really attracted you?

This was in the 1950s. There wasn't much literature on Buddhism in English at that time. The book I found, *The Way of Zen*, by Alan Watts, presented a path of insight and inquiry, especially into the nature of my self and my world. That was very comfortable and interesting to me. It meant that I did not have to accept particular beliefs, which was very freeing. It said that a person was expected to discover truth for oneself through personal experience. And as I read further I was very much taken by the teachings on meditation as a path to self-discovery. The teachings on loving kindness and compassion were very meaningful to me as well.

How did you go about finding out more about Buddhism when there was so little information available then?

Well, that was the problem. In the 1950s there were very few books and no Buddhist centers, temples; or teachers for me to turn to. It was hard to find accurate, authentic information on Buddhism. Of course today all that has changed. In the 1960s many of us who were interested in Buddhism went to India to meet authentic Buddhist teachers. We learned the languages, and started translating Buddhist texts into English and inviting Buddhist teachers to North America. Now, as a result of that, there are Buddhist centers in every major city in the United States, and plenty of books available about Buddhism and the Buddhist teachings.

But at the time, before you found any of these things, did you consider yourself truly Buddhist?

Karma Lekshe Tsomo

Yes. I remember from the age of about eleven feeling in my heart that I had taken refuge, which is the distinguishing characteristic of being a Buddhist. We take refuge in the Buddha, in his teachings, and in the spiritual community of those who are dedicated to achieving enlightenment.

And did you find that community of other people devoted to achieving enlightenment?

No! Not at the time. I was sitting in my room meditating and wondering, "Where is everybody?" It was a pretty isolating experience. I felt quite alienated from mainstream belief systems, and I had to strike out on my own individual path. To do that well, you need reliable sources of information, and there were very few. Because of this I went to Asia when I was nineteen.

Did you immediately find what you were looking for?

While I was on a surfing trip to Japan in 1964, I started meditating, but I didn't find a teacher there, so I traveled on to India and Nepal. I was really looking for a monastery, because I wanted to become a Buddhist nun. I wanted to practice Buddhism seriously. But I didn't find a monastery for women in any of the places I went to. I found many for monks, but nothing for nuns.

Why were there no monasteries for women?

The problem is simply that most societies, until very recently, have tended to privilege men. The education systems and religious institutions offer many opportunities to boys and men. But women have fewer opportunities because society has assumed for so long that marriage and motherhood are the goals for all women. Today that is changing, and women have many more opportunities than before. But when I was growing up, it was assumed that women would get married and have a family. I simply was not interested in that role, which is why I was looking at other religious traditions. I was looking for something that offered an alternative to traditional expectations. I wanted to concentrate on spiritual development, and Buddhism offered that option. But even there opportunities for women were not equal to those for men. This is why I became involved in the Buddhist women's movement.

Was the Buddhist community welcoming to you?

In the beginning I was too shy to approach people. I didn't even know what questions to ask. I learned some basic Buddhist teachings, and I kept reading books on Buddhism. But when I went into monasteries, I was hesitant to ask people to sit down and explain things to me.

Karma Lekshe Tsomo

Now I find people very friendly, but at the time I was young and rather reserved.

Also, Buddhism is not a faith that evangelizes or tries to draw people into it, correct?

That's right. It's a journey. The search for a teacher or spiritual home is a search for a path with which you have a karmic affinity. Buddhists do not try to recruit people or entice them to join. It's believed that when a person is ready to find a teacher or a community, those things will appear.

You made a literal journey, traveling around the world trying to find your path. What was it like when you finally found people to give you the information you were after?

It was like coming home. Buddhism felt comfortable and familiar. But of course then there were language problems. In the end I learned all of these different languages so that I could speak to people and read the texts in their original languages: Japanese, Tibetan, and Chinese. My generation, the first generation of Western people to seek out Buddhist teachings, really had to work at it.

At what point did you decide that you wanted to spend your life in Buddhism?

I knew very early on that this was my path. But there is quite a distance between recognizing your path and making a lifelong commitment to it. Worldly affairs are always vying for our attention. Things like profession, education, relationships, and other different interests. I did many things, including tai chi, painting, aikido, yoga, poetry, music, and surfing. For me, learning to balance the spiritual with the worldly was the first step. Then, later, I gradually realized that in order to really concentrate on spiritual practice, I needed to simplify my life. I couldn't do all of these other things *and* concentrate on meditation. I knew I had to make some choices. I had to make spirituality central and the other interests peripheral.

Did you ever consider going the other way and choosing the world?

I was never interested in a career, family life, or anything like that. So it wasn't a difficult choice from that perspective. But there were things I had to let go of, which wasn't always easy. You get sucked into things, like relationships, that get very complicated.

Does being a Buddhist mean that someone has to give up all those things?

The path of a nun or monk is an ascetic path, but it isn't necessary to be a monk or a nun to be a Buddhist.

Karma Lekshe Tsomo

It just so happened that I felt inclined toward the monastic path. I was attracted to meditation, learning, and a simple monastic life. But most Buddhists are family people, and it is certainly possible to be a Buddhist and have those things. You can do meditation in the comfort of your own home; you don't need to be in a monastery. The important thing is developing mindfulness, compassion, loving kindness, and wisdom. We can do all of these things whether we are living in a family or in a monastery. The practice is basically the same. It's very rare, actually, that a person decides to choose the monastic life. It's not an easy path. It does mean giving up a lot of what the world calls fun and what the world sees as important.

When you were first in India and looking for places to go study as a woman, were the teachers open to that idea, or was the feeling that you should be happy with what you got?

I was very fortunate because by the time I returned to India, in 1972, His Holiness the Dalai Lama had founded the Tibetan Library, a place in Dharmsala where Western women and men could study Buddhism. For higher studies, however, opportunities were limited. Eventually I founded a monastery to provide educational opportunities for Himalayan women. At that time many people simply didn't recognize the imbalance that existed between monastic opportunities for women and for men.

Conditions were very difficult because so many Tibetan Buddhist monks and nuns were living in India as refugees after the Communist Chinese takeover of Tibet, which destroyed more than six thousand monasteries. More than one hundred thousand people, including many monks and nuns, escaped to India and were working under conditions of extreme poverty to re-create the religious institutions that had existed in Tibet. Resources were very limited.

What was the response when you founded the monastery?

At first there was some opposition. Many people were comfortable with things as they were and resisted change. It's not easy to start something new.

Many people have the idea that Buddhism is an ideal religion, all about peace and tranquility. Is that a misconception on the part of westerners looking at an Eastern religion?

Buddhism is about peace and tranquility. But like in any religion, not all Buddhists follow Buddhist principles all of the time.

How do you deal with situations where what you want is in conflict with what others in your religion think is right?

Well, that's what meditation is all about. Buddhist meditation is a tool for dealing with conflicting emotions,

Karma Lekshe Tsomo

such as anger, attachment, pride, and jealousy, all the emotions that human beings have. Buddhist meditation provides specific techniques for dealing with negative emotions. Why do we get angry? Who is it that's getting angry? These are the questions we can address through meditation. Buddhism also provides techniques for developing loving kindness, so that instead of responding with anger, we respond with patience, love, and compassion. Meditation provides innumerable techniques for dealing with the problems of daily life, and I've found those techniques to be very helpful in the challenging work that I do.

Okay, but aren't there still days when you want to tell off a few people who really make you mad?

Laughing Well, that is not my way. I do feel hurt and wronged sometimes. But basic to the Buddhist world view is a new way of looking at self-identity. In the Western traditions, creating an individual self with our own likes and dislikes, and our own personality, is a cultural ideal. Each one of us begins, from a young age, to carve out a special, individual, personal identity unique to ourselves. But in Buddhism this is not the goal. The goal is to look at that concept of self and realize that it causes us a lot of problems. Differentiating one's self from others, and assuming that my benefit is more important than the benefit of others, is a mistake, an illusion. Where do we get the idea that we are more important than others? Everyone else has the same aspirations to happiness, and everyone else is trying to avoid pain and problems, so we're all actually the same in that. By assuming that I am more important than someone else, I am beginning with a mistaken belief, and that's where problems begin. So when someone challenges my ideas or otherwise does wrong to me, I try to stay calm and use reason to figure out a solution. When we begin to see the self in a new light and understand the problems caused by clinging to individual identity, we begin to cut through that solid sense of self that causes us to cling to things and suffer when we don't get what we want.

But that's incredibly difficult to do in a world that continually tells you that achieving your own goals is what is really important.

Exactly, and that's why Buddhism provides an alternative to the ordinary way of looking at the world that causes so many problems.

Buddhism has become incredibly popular in America. Do you find any irony in the fact that a religion that began among people who are very poor, and which is based on not being attached to the things of the world, is now being practiced by a great many people with very comfortable lives who lack very little in the way of material things?

Karma Lekshe Tsomo   79

That's actually very natural. If people are not finding happiness even with so many material possessions, they are likely to seek spiritual solutions. This is also one of the things that led me to work with social action. Buddhism will be interpreted differently in the West than in Asia because of our different cultural background. For example, most accounts of Buddhism in the West focus almost entirely on the Euro-American experience. Very little attention has been given to Asian Buddhism in America or to Asian-American Buddhism in America. Buddhism is definitely being understood and practiced differently in America than it has been understood and practiced in Asia.

Do you think Buddhism is a religion, or is it simply a philosophy?

That is a point of great debate. I think that people even within Buddhism have different opinions. Some consider it a philosophy. Some consider it a way of life. Many dispute that it matches the traditional definition of a religion. Some people may also practice it in ways that would qualify it as a religion. It depends upon how one defines religion.

Let's say you define religion as a set of spiritual directions you follow to get yourself to a certain place when you die.

Then Buddhism might qualify as a religion. Buddhism talks a lot about death. And that was the thread of my early questioning—what happens to us after death. Eventually, when I came to Buddhism, especially in the Tibetan tradition, I found that there is a very elaborate technology of dying. It presents the stages of the dying process and how to handle all of those stages, and how to die peacefully and constructively. That moment of death is seen, by Buddhists, as the most important moment of one's life. In many ways one's life is seen as preparation for that moment. If we prepare to die well, we'll find that we are also prepared to live well.

The Buddhist tradition also teaches that essentially all life is suffering. Don't you find that a little depressing?

Let's say it's a matter of looking at life realistically. We are always running into problems. Instead of getting upset about these things, Buddhists learn to accept that problems are simply part and parcel of living, that all people experience these kinds of problems, especially the problems of birth, sickness, old age, and death. But for many people these problems don't come about until later in life, so we blissfully ignore them. Then when they come up, we don't know how to cope with them. I think the Buddhist approach is more realistic. We understand that these problems are not necessarily depressing; they are just practical matters. There's no guarantee that we will be sick or die only when we are old. Sickness or death can happen at any time, either to ourselves or to the people around us, so we need to learn how to cope with them.

And these aren't the only problems. There are also problems of not getting what we want or getting what we don't want. People often think, "Why me?" when these things happen. But the Buddhists explain it through the concept of karma, the law of cause and effect. We believe that we experience happiness and unhappiness as a result of our own actions in this and in other lifetimes. We believe that wholesome actions of body, speech, and mind bring us happiness both in this lifetime and in the future.

Is your next life something you consciously think about?

Buddhists in many countries do think about it. For example, when you see women in Thailand or Sri Lanka offering food to the monks, they are definitely thinking about gaining what they call merit for future lives. It is widely believed that wholesome actions in this life will produce happiness for oneself and others, whether in this life or future ones. Whether we accept the theory of karma or not, our positive deeds in this life will ripen as happiness in the future. Whether that happiness will come in the same lifetime or in other lifetimes, we cannot say, but the important thing is to engage in wholesome actions like generosity, ethical behavior, patience, joyful effort, meditation, and wisdom. All of these

Paths of Faith

positive actions definitely make us happy now, and maybe in future lives as well.

Earlier you mentioned that your social work came out of your spiritual searching. Do you think that is a natural effect?

If we try to develop compassion in ourselves, then it's natural that the compassion should express itself in creating benefit for society. Compassionate social action is a natural extension of our personal practice of meditation. To me, these two go hand in hand.

Where, for you, is the line between being involved with the affairs of the world and being removed from the cares of the world?

That's a dance. I strive to achieve a balance between meditation, learning, and social action. The needs of the world are great, so the social action side always has a tendency to take over. I have to very conscientiously set aside time for two hours of formal spiritual practice, such as meditation, every day. That's how I more or less recharge the batteries in order to work effectively in society. Because the needs of sentient beings are endless, we could pass out lunch on the street every day, but it wouldn't necessarily solve the problem. The problem of why some people go hungry lies far deeper than that. From a Buddhist point of view, we need to get at the root of what causes these problems, meaning we need to

Karma Lekshe Tsomo

personally do good deeds to assure happy results for ourselves in the future, and encourage other people to do good deeds as well. We need to avoid unwholesome actions ourselves and help others to avoid unwholesome actions as well.

When would that come into conflict? For example, do you involve yourself in politics and vote?

Sure. If we care about society, then we definitely have to make our voices heard. The other way that Buddhist practice is important in social activism is that when we get involved in social-action projects, whether they be environmental, political, or whatever, conflicts may arise among people. Buddhist practice is very beneficial in dealing with interpersonal relationships and for dealing effectively with the feelings that arise when we engage in social activism. People become angry about injustice, the indignities and inequities. That is natural. But if we can develop a peaceful heart, we can deal with very difficult situations more calmly and more constructively. That is the benefit of grounding our social-action efforts in Buddhist practice.

Do you think Buddhist practice can help anyone who tries it?

Sure. You don't have to be Buddhist to do Buddhist practice. There are techniques for developing loving kindness and mindfulness that many Christians and people of other faiths are using today. Many followers of other religions are learning mindfulness meditation and Zen meditation and finding that these practices not only complement their own personal religious practice but also enhance it. If we learn how to send loving kindness instead of anger when we feel ourselves becoming upset, then we can transform the negative emotion of anger into a positive one of compassion. Obviously, a person who is angry is suffering. Perhaps she's having a terrible day. Instead of returning that anger with more anger, we can transform it into loving kindness.

That's easy to say, but putting it into practice is often very difficult.

It *is* difficult sometimes. It takes a great deal of practice to develop patience, wisdom, and loving kindness. We also have to find appropriate ways to express that loving kindness. Sometimes it can just be visualized internally. Sometimes we will actually take action to help another person. We have to learn what is appropriate in each situation.

Can you think of anything you would fight for?

Definitely, but not in a violent way. I believe that violence is counterproductive. There are usually other ways to deal with violent or unacceptable situations.

Karma Lekshe Tsomo

Many Tibetan Buddhists have been killed in Chinese-occupied Tibet because of that belief. How do you explain to someone looking at that situation from the outside that those sacrifices are not in vain?

If we return violence with violence, there's a danger of killing someone and escalating the violence. The effects of killing another human being, or any living being, extend far beyond this life into other lifetimes. Killing is also risky because it often incites more killing, continuing in an endless downward spiral. Violence only expands the further it goes. It also affects our future lives by causing negative consequences in future rebirths. Whether or not we accept the idea of rebirth, suffering is the natural outcome of killing. If we can learn nonviolent communication skills, we can learn how to solve conflicts constructively. Patience and loving kindness serve as antidotes to violence, and confrontations naturally decrease. Nonviolent solutions are by far the most effective way to deal with situations. Situations of political oppression are very difficult to handle. There's no question about that. But a violent response to oppression, I maintain, is counterproductive. This is the message of spiritual leaders such as His Holiness the Dalai Lama.

Can you explain what you mean by the effects extending into other lifetimes?

It's like dropping a stone into water. The ripples continue to radiate out from the center, getting larger and larger. In the same way, the effects of violence ripple out, becoming larger and larger. But the effects of meditation, loving kindness, and compassionate social action also ripple out. If we are able to deal with conflict in a loving way, we also have the power to transform some very nasty, very violent situations through our spiritual practice. We can deal with situations on a different level. It doesn't have to be about guns. Loving kindness is the most powerful weapon there is. It can be totally transformative.

You mentioned at the beginning of our discussion the fact that you saw a lot of hypocrisy in the churches you grew up in. Have you seen any of that in the Buddhist tradition as you've walked your path?

The teachings that the Buddha gave us are all meant to be tested and verified through our own experience. There are no teachings that we are expected to accept without question. We can try out the teachings in our daily life and find out whether they work or not. How each person practices is a matter of personal responsibility. Our first responsibility is to improve the quality of our own actions. This is a full-time job. Our task is not to critique the actions of others or stand in judgment of others. We have the freedom, and in a sense the responsibility, to talk with people if we feel that they are harming others, but primarily our individual responsibility is to improve the quality of our own actions and become an example. Buddhists strive to embody the teachings of the Buddha, but we are not always successful. When we are, hopefully we will be inspiring to others.

FOR MORE INFORMATION

ON-LINE RESOURCES

BuddhaNet: Buddhist Information Network
www.buddhanet.net

One of the most comprehensive sites about Buddhism on the Net, BuddhaNet provides links to many different organizations, periodicals, and other Web sites having to do with Buddhism.

DharmaNet International
www.dharmanet.org

In addition to links to general Buddhist interest sites, DharmaNet provides information about Buddhist teachers, classes, and teaching centers around the world. It's a great resource if you want to find a Buddhist center near you.

Sakyadhita: The International Association of Buddhist Women
www2.hawaii.edu/~tsomo

This organization was founded by Karma Lekshe Tsomo and friends. It is a wonderful place to find information about the role of women in Buddhism and about the different options available to women who want to study the tradition more thoroughly.

BOOKS

It's Easier Than You Think: The Buddhist Way to Happiness, by Sylvia Boorstein (HarperSanFrancisco, 1997). One of the clearest, most accessible introductions to Buddhist teachings and practices.

Freedom in Exile: The Autobiography of the Dalai Lama, by Tenzin Gyatso (HarperCollins, 1990). This is the amazing and inspiring life story of the Fourteenth Dalai Lama of Tibet, probably the most recognized figure in Buddhism, from his childhood through his dramatic escape from Chinese-occupied Tibet.

Buddhism Plain and Simple, by Steven Hagen (Broadway Books, 1998). A basic, easy-to-understand introduction to the beliefs and practices of the religion.

Awakening the Buddha Within: Tibetan Wisdom for the Western World, by Lama Surya Das (Broadway Books, 1998). Lama Surya Das is an American who has spent many years studying in the Buddhist tradition. He is considered one of the finest Buddhist teachers in the West, and his many books are wonderful explorations of what it means to be a Buddhist and how Buddhist teachings can be used by anyone.

Buddhism through American Women's Eyes, by Karma Lekshe Tsomo (Snow Lion Publications, 1995). A collection of essays in which American Buddhist women discuss how being part of the religion has had an impact on their life.

Awakening the Mind: Basic Buddhist Meditations, by Geshe Namgyal Wangchen (Wisdom Publications, 1995). A fine introduction to the art of meditation.

The Way of Zen, by Alan Watts (Vintage Books, 1998). This is the book that first brought Karma Lekshe Tsomo into Buddhism. Considered a classic, it is one of the most influential books on Zen Buddhism.

The Right Reverend
John Shelby Spong, D.D.
Bishop, the Episcopal Diocese of Newark

"If God is the source of love, then I reveal God by being capable of giving love away. If God is the source of life, then I reveal God by living fully. To me, to live and to love and to be is what the Christian life is."

The Episcopal Church has its roots in the Church of England, and its history is strongly tied to the political history of that country. Since before the fourth century England has been a largely Christian nation, and for more than twelve hundred years the church in England had a stormy relationship with what is now called the Roman Catholic Church, depending on the religious views of the monarch who ruled at the time. Some British rulers favored the Catholic Church, while others wished to see an independent national church of England, free of papal control.

In the sixteenth century the division between the two churches widened when the archbishop of Canterbury, the Right Reverend Thomas Cranmer, created the first Book of Common Prayer, which was written in English, the common language of the people, and designed to be used by the people. Until that time the church liturgy was conducted in Latin, which few people understood, and only clergy were allowed to read the Scriptures. At this time the Bible was also translated into English and made available to all people.

The schism between the churches was made worse by the actions of King Henry VIII, who disobeyed and angered the pope by taking a series of wives in an attempt at producing a male heir. That heir, Edward VI, supported an independent Church of England. But upon his death his half sister Mary I came to the throne. A staunch Roman Catholic, Mary tried to purge the English church of its independence by ordering the burning of priests, including Archbishop Cranmer. When Mary was deposed, Henry's daughter Elizabeth I came to power. Elizabeth, opposed to Catholicism, engineered what is known as the Elizabethan Settlement, which defined the Church of England as an independent national church.

The Church of England came to America in 1607 with the establishment of the Jamestown Colony and the arrival of the first Church of England priest in the New World, the Reverend Robert Hunt. The church

Paths of Faith

grew in popularity, and its members and clergy were instrumental in organizing the American Revolution of 1776. George Washington was a vestryman of an Anglican church, as were most of the chaplains of the Continental army. When the war was over, however, there was a great backlash against the church because of the fact that it had been the established church of England, and property belonging to the church was seized.

The church remained intact, however, and by the beginning of the nineteenth century had formed itself into a nationwide church that called itself Episcopal, meaning "led by shepherds," referring to the bishops who were the heads of the church. It also maintained a loose connection to the mother church in England, which continues to this day.

Bishop John Shelby Spong is one of the most controversial, influential, and interesting characters in the Episcopal Church. A priest since 1955, he was consecrated a bishop of the diocese of Newark, New Jersey, in 1976. Bishop Spong has written numerous books about spiritual topics, and has been at the forefront of getting the church to address issues such as the ordination of women and the acceptance of lesbian and gay people. He is one of the most visible examples of someone who has remained within a spiritual tradition he is sometimes at odds with, while attempting to create change in that tradition.

*What was your relationship to spirituality when you were grow-
ing up?*

I've always had a love affair with the church, and I
don't quite understand where it comes from. I can
remember, even as a little kid of five or six, playing
church. I would play Communion. In my later teenage
years I became very active in the youth group of my diocese. I would go to camp in the summer with other
young people from the church, and they became my
close group of friends outside of school. I was later
elected president of the youth group, and I traveled a lot
to speak to youth groups all over the diocese. It was an
extended family to me.

I also loved the Bible. When I was in high school, I
took two courses in Bible, which was still being taught
in public schools at that time. This was 1948 or 1949.
My teacher loved the Bible, and she would tell these
magnificent stories that held me mesmerized, stories
about the apostle Paul or about David and Goliath. I've
read the Bible every day of my life from the time I was
twelve years old.

What kept you there as you grew older?

When I was twelve years old, I actually changed
churches, but it was not over any feelings of dissatisfac-
tion. It was because I joined a boys choir at another

Episcopal church. There was no choir in the church I went to, so I began to go to this other church, where I had a wonderful choirmaster. Choir was very important to me. We had rehearsal every Wednesday afternoon and every Saturday morning. We got paid fifty cents a month to sing in that choir. From time to time we were asked to sing at weddings. All of this made us feel very important.

My father died during that time, and my choirmaster became something of a father to me. More important, a couple of years later we got a new priest in our church. He was thirty-two years old. I didn't think a priest could be that young; I thought they all had to be about eighty. He was a very alive, affirming person. He was married to a lovely woman. They had no children, and he kind of adopted me in the same way that I adopted him.

At that point being an acolyte in the church was important to me. I became the acolyte who would always attend the 8 A.M. service and serve at the altar. The priest was a terribly important person to me. I loved that man, and I loved him because he took time to listen to me. He was the only adult in my teenage years who ever listened to me or spoke *with* me instead of to me or at me. He listened to my responses. We would eat breakfast together every Sunday morning, and I wanted to be like that man more than I wanted to be like anyone else. He was the source of what was my first interest in becoming a priest.

The Right Reverend John Shelby Spong, D.D.   95

*Did you connect any of these experiences with God or with spiritu-
ality, or were they primarily about feeling respected?*

My early upbringing was in biblical Fundamentalism of the evangelical southern tradition. My mother
was an Associate Reform Presbyterian, a very strict
Fundamentalist type of group. To them everything was
all black and white. That gave me a certain amount of
security. I thought I had all the answers. There were no
gray areas in my life. God was very much a superparent
up in the sky who demanded certain things of me, all of
which were interpreted in terms of things you did or did
not do. You didn't smoke. You didn't drink. You didn't
dance. You didn't do anything that was "bad," because
God was always watching.

Did you agree with that view?

I moved out of Fundamentalism when I was fourteen or fifteen years old because what I was learning
in school made a Fundamentalist attitude toward the
Bible nonsensical to me. Things like the belief that
the prophet Joshua stopped the Sun in the middle of
the sky, when in fact the Sun does not revolve around
Earth, Earth revolves around the Sun. And the whole
Darwinian theory of evolution, which challenged the
version of the creation of the world given in Genesis.
Those were the kinds of things that made me question

the Fundamentalist view of the Bible as completely literal.

Did that make you question the whole notion of Christianity?

The new rector who came to mean so much to me was sort of what we call an Anglo-Catholic. He didn't quote the Bible. He simply said, "The church teaches us that this or that is true," and that was his final authority, much as it is in the Catholic tradition. In order not to lose my faith, which was being questioned by these things I was learning in school, I became an Anglo-Catholic as well. The view there is that truth is not what the Bible says literally, but what the church historically has taught about it over the years. It was another kind of Fundamentalism, but I didn't recognize that at the time. At a young age I really did believe that truth was what the church said it was.

Your views now are certainly not like the things you were taught early on or like those of the rector who influenced you. When did they change?

They changed in seminary. And they changed, I think, in a very positive direction. That's where I gave up the Anglo-Catholic notion that the church was the final authority on spiritual matters. I had already given up the Fundamentalist idea of a black-and-white authority system. But at that point I gave up the Anglo-Catholic idea as well and started on the path I still am on. I would describe it as a journey into the mystery of God. It doesn't have any boundaries, and the road isn't always clearly marked. One simply is open to the journeying experience.

How did that change your own spirituality?

God, for me, became more and more real, and less and less describable in words. Other people were very important to me during that time. One was John A. T. Robinson, the bishop and theologian, who became my mentor and friend after I read his book *Honest to God.* Through friendships with people like John, it was a wonderful experience for me to begin to probe areas of my faith's tradition and to try to make sense out of it in a contemporary world.

You became a priest at a time in the country's history when social and political events were very much challenging spiritual beliefs. The civil rights movement, for example, was a big challenge to many churches. How did that affect you?

It enhanced my spirituality greatly. At that time I was greatly influenced by the work of Bishop John E. Hines. John was so totally clear about the fact that the gospel must be lived out in terms of justice. Worship is nothing except justice being offered to God, and justice is nothing but worship being lived out. That was a concept that John taught, and it was very clear to him. He called the whole church into living that out.

When the desegregation order came down, I had to put my body in place in that movement. It was a very dramatic and very exciting time. It wasn't always easy, but it was invigorating. At the time, I was in a little town in North Carolina that was 50 percent black. I served in a black church in a very segregated world. It was one block away from the white church. That really did educate me. It was wonderful, and I love that little church to this day. It's still there, even though that little town has become much more integrated over the years.

The war in Vietnam also captured my attention and demanded a response. Then it was the role of women in the life of both church and society that really demanded action. My sense of justice was addressed toward the issue of ordaining women and opening up the whole of society for women. Then, when I was elected bishop in 1976, for the first time in my life I was confronted with the issue of serving a visible gay community. So I have been involved in many different areas of social change over the years.

The issue of gay men and lesbians within the church is one that you have become very well known for addressing. How did that happen?

I'm sure there were always gay people in the communities that I served, but they were not visible. Then, when I came to this diocese, I found a very strong, self-accepting gay community. There are also many clergy who are gay. When I moved here, I had to embrace that. And it was not easy for me, because I was still operating under the stereotype and definition of gay people as being mentally ill or having chosen to live a depraved or immoral life. I had to address those misconceptions. Now, I suppose that when I retire, that will be the thing that most people remember, because it's the most controversial topic I've ever become involved in.

Do you think that challenging your faith and deciding for yourself what it means is a necessary thing?

My belief is that your faith will not survive if you don't challenge it. When I look at young people who do not examine their faith, I see that they become sort of religious robots. When I look at those who do examine their faith, I see them so discouraged by the state of institutionalized religion that they're in effect made to feel that they are no longer part of the Christian community. I find today's young people to be religiously fascinated but not particularly church oriented. That's a distinction I think is very clear.

For myself, it took a long time to break the symbols of my faith open and see what they held for me. But what I've come to understand is that there's a big difference between the experience of God and the description of that experience. What the church has done as an institution is to elevate the description of the experience into an authoritarian system that tells people, "This is the way things are," rather than, "This is the description of the experience that we have had historically."

Can you give an example of that?

The various creeds we follow, for example, do not capture the truth of God. The best that the creeds do is tell us how people in the fourth and fifth centuries processed their Christian faith in the light of the world that they were living in. That's true even of the Bible. Once you get really deep into the gospel tradition, you recognize first that there was a remarkable Jewish influence on the way Jesus was understood.

For example, we call Jesus "the Lamb of God," which is an image that comes out of the Jewish tradition of Yom Kippur. But most Christians have no idea what that tradition is, so they end up just saying the words without really understanding what they might signify. The idea that Christ is the new sacrificial lamb of Yom Kippur, whose blood takes away the sins of the world, might have made sense in a Jewish community that understood the tradition of Yom Kippur. But when you take it out of that community, it turns God into a barbarian who kills

The Right Reverend John Shelby Spong, D.D.   101

his son in order to have a sacrifice that will enable himself to forgive.

That's not the kind of God I would want to worship. But those images are so deep in the Christian tradition, and they are unchallenged and unexplained because most people, religious leaders included, do not know what the roots of those ideas are. To me, the experience of God is incredibly real. But the explanation of the experience is always limited. It's bound by the time in which the person telling the story lived. What I feel compelled to do today is to try to find a way to put my experience of God into language that is nontraditional, language that my generation can at least hear and respond to. Whether I am successful or not is another issue, but that's what my motivation is.

Yet many traditions, especially Fundamentalist Christian traditions, actively discourage people from questioning their faith. So how do young people who have issues with things in their particular faith work to change those things?

Change might not be the right word. What I try to do in my own faith is try to understand what the experience was that caused a person to describe that experience with God in the way he or she did. Then I try to see if I can keep the experience but find a new way to talk about it. To me, that's a crucial distinction. I have a real love affair with my church, but the church has also come closer to killing me than any other institution you can imagine. The church is much more interested in propaganda than it is in education.

I am impressed by a poster I saw on a church wall one day that said, "Why is it that churches that claim to have all the answers don't allow any questions?" That's a good question. When I talk to young people, including my own children, I find them searching for some sort of ultimate meaning, some sort of relationship with God, but not finding anything in the church that they are particularly attracted to. Many of them are so turned off by their idea of what Christianity is that they cannot even connect with it at all. They are looking for something, but what they're being offered isn't something they can grab on to.

Many people, especially young people, do wonder what the point of exploring spirituality is. What do you think it is?

I think the point of it is that in the relationship of a human being with God, the human being explodes into the fullness of her or his humanity. When I think of God now, I use the definition of God as the ground of all being. That means that I reveal God the more fully I am capable of being myself. If God is the source of love, then I reveal God by being capable of giving love away. If God is the source of life, then I reveal God by living fully. To me, to live and to love and to be is what the Christian life is.

The Right Reverend John Shelby Spong, D.D.   103

The reason that I maintain my Christian identity is that when I look at Jesus and hear people make the God claim for him, I say, "What definition of God are we claiming is present in Jesus?" If it's the definition of God as the source of life, then I see the fullness of life in Jesus. If it's the definition of God as the source of all love, I see the perfect love of God being manifested in Jesus. And if it's the God who is the ground of all being, I see Jesus being all that he is capable of at every stage of his life, whether they're cheering him as the king on Palm Sunday or killing him on Good Friday. Whatever the situation, he is still a full being who is able to give his life away. I locate the godlikeness in Jesus in those things that I think are the same places where I located God in myself.

Do you think all people can become like Jesus?

I would agree with my friend John Robinson when he said that the only difference between Jesus and me is a difference of degree, and not of kind. It's officially heresy in the church, but I think it's dead right. It means that what Jesus reveals is the God presence that is in all the world and in all of us, and that he reveals it perfectly in a way that I can reveal only inadequately. That's why he is *the* Christ for me, but I am *a* Christ in the sense that I am the conduit through which other people meet the love of God. So is every other

Christian. It's taking the "ground of being" concept of God and running it through the system so that being and God are correlated. Not that God is a being who is external to life and periodically invades our lives, but that God is the very substance of life, the source of life, and that this God is being revealed in and through the Creation at all times and was uniquely revealed in the life of Jesus of Nazareth, which enables me to see the God who is present in all of life all the time.

How do you see the traditional Christian concept of Christ's death being necessary to "save" people from sin?

I think we need to change that. I think we have to get away from the image of God as a potentate who demands sacrifice in order to overcome the brokenness of the human relationship. In some sense Charles Darwin put an end to that with his theory of evolution. What the church myth says is that there was a perfect creation from which humans, by an act of disobedience, fell into sin. We could not rescue ourselves, so we necessitated a divine rescuer. Then Jesus is the divine rescuer who comes into the broken world, suffers the consequences, and dies on the cross in order to lift us back into what God had intended us to be all the time. I grew up with that idea, and so do millions upon millions of people. It permeates the Sacraments. It permeates the Scriptures.

The Right Reverend John Shelby Spong, D.D.

It's a standard way that Christians have interpreted reality.

But Darwin said something different. He said that there never was a perfect creation. You cannot fall from perfection if you've never achieved it. What we are is a work in progress. We are an emerging consciousness. I don't mean that sin isn't real. Sin is real. But sin, to me, is the vestigial remains of an evolutionary process that demanded that we be radically self-centered in order to survive.

How so?

If the law of the jungle is survival of the fittest, every person seeks to be the fittest. That means every person enters life from a vantage point of total self-centeredness. If there are two people left and only one bone, survival will demand that one of those two people kills the other and gets the bone. That's the nature of humanity, and it's the burden and the baggage that we carry. That's what the church has identified as sin and thought of as the fall from grace. I think of it as the inadequacy of a still-evolving species.

What the Christian faith does for me is present me with an image of the infinite love of God. If I can touch that love, the life-giving quality of love that I see in Jesus, then I can be called beyond all of my boundaries, including the boundary that puts my survival at the center of my life.

Have you been able to experience that?

I can only get a taste of that. I love my wife so totally and so dearly. She is the most wonderful creature in the world. I would willingly and happily die for her if that's the choice I had to face. I love her enough to give everything that I am to her, including my life if it were required. My sense is that's a new level of humanity, that's a new evolution of my spirit to a point where I can so deeply love someone that I give up all of my desires to survive and to struggle, which are basic human desires. That, to me, is what the fullness of humanity is all about. If I can achieve that with my wife, and perhaps with my children, then perhaps I can extend that to others. If I can do it with people who are such deep sources of love, perhaps I can then expand it to people beyond that source of love.

Isn't that what you do when you advocate for the rights of others, or when you call for the acceptance of all people?

In terms of the work I've done in the church, it all comes out of that belief that I have to get past my prejudices against black people as inferior creatures, my definition of a woman as simply the helpmate of a male, my stereotype of gay and lesbian people as depraved parts of humanity. I have to recognize that all people are different aspects of humanity. They might not be my aspect, but they are an aspect that has always been part of the human equation. You must accept that and affirm it and love it beyond its boundaries too.

The job of the Christian Church is not to tell people whether they're right or wrong, or to control behavior. The job of the Christian Church, for me, is to proclaim the infinite love of God so that people can touch that love and escape their boundaries and their barriers and their insecurities and their willingness to hurt others out of their need instead of being willing to give their lives away out of their fullness. That's what I'm trying to communicate to people. It's what is behind my books. It's what is behind my life. It's what makes me the "controversial" bishop of Newark.

On issues where you have had to change your own personal views, such as the ordination of women or the acceptance of lesbian and gay people, how hard has that been?

To me it was a growing experience. What I basically had to lay down were my prejudices, in order to act upon new knowledge. I'm a person who has to think his way into new ways of acting. Before I wrote anything on homosexuality, for example, I went to Cornell Medical Center in New York. I worked with the doctors there and tried to read everything I could read that would help me understand intellectually that gay people are a normal minority aspect of the human spectrum of sexuality. It's not abnormal, it's just a minority. I had to come to the awareness that homo-sexuality is a given and not a chosen. And, for me, that knowledge meant that we had to develop a whole new ethical system for embracing gay people, rather than holding them accountable for what they were created to be. I knew that we had to find a way for gay and lesbian people to live out who they were supposed to be in ways that are life affirming. That's why I support the church blessing the committed relationships of gay and lesbian people, because I think gay people have the same rights that heterosexual people do to form sacred, bonded, committed relationships. But that demands coming up with a different definition of gay people than many people are conditioned to have. And changing that definition, both on a personal level and on a larger, society-wide level, is hard.

Then where is the line between logical thinking and having faith on spiritual issues?

Once again, I think that we have to recognize that every theological word, every biblical word, represents an attempt on the part of our ancestors in faith to make sense out of a God experience in their time and place. The experience, I believe, is eternal and real. The explanation will never be eternal and real. It will last only as long as the mind-set that created it. I think the only ulti-mate truth is that God is real, and that we experience the reality of God. Then we have to talk about it. And when we talk about it, we immediately put it into our vocabulary, our mind-set, our frame of reference, and our level of knowledge.

When we defined God as a being above the sky, we assumed that there was a three-tiered universe and heaven was just above the sky and God was a being that periodically invaded this world to manipulate life. It's hard to take that point of view and be on this side of scientific truth and take it seriously. Does that mean that the whole God experience of early people ought to be thrown out? No. But many people have done that. They look at these questions, see that the church belief doesn't make sense regarding them, and they throw it out altogether. Fundamentalists say that the church, and the gospel, are all still true whether you understand it or not. They claim it's just a matter of believing properly. What I'm trying to say is that the experience that created the Gospels is true. The experience that created the creeds is true. But neither the Gospels nor the creeds can fully capture that experience for all time. They captured it only for their time in history. I want to take that seriously.

But does that mean just throwing out tradition and coming up with new ones?

No. There are churches that do that, but I don't think it's entirely useful. I want to wrestle with tradition and see what is inside it. I don't want just to throw it away, because it might need to be reexamined.

I think there's an awful lot in religion that's neurotic. And I think also that if your religion makes you feel secure about everything, deep down it's probably a neurotic faith. What Christianity does for me is not to make me secure, but to give me the courage to live in a radically insecure world as a radically insecure person, knowing that God is always in front of me, behind me, and beside me. I walk into the unknown constantly because I have confidence that God is in that unknown.

You've frequently butted heads with people within your own tradition. How do you handle those times when you know that what you're fighting for is right but everyone is telling you you're wrong?

I live pretty much in peace with the church on that issue, because my sense is that if the church ever got to the place where it couldn't stand to have people like me in it—people who are raising questions and challenging old formulas and trying to find new ways to say things—then that would be a sign that the church had died, and I wouldn't want to be a part of it anyway. God would have to raise up another community where God's life and love could be manifested.

The church is a sign of the kingdom of God; therefore, as I see it, it should be impossible for the church to be bigoted on issues of racism or chauvinism or homo-phobia, because if we are, we are violating the very thing that we are about. Those are not liberal causes that I march to because I am a liberal. Those are gospel issues that are at the heart of my understanding of what God is all about.

My understanding of God, and the God in Christ, is that there is nothing that you or I could ever do or be that would separate us from the love of God. Even when you kill the love of God, God responds by loving you. That's what I see in the gospel and in the story of Jesus. So I cannot live that story out if I am homophobic or if I say that women are second-class citizens or if I believe that blacks ought to be segregated. Those ways of think-ing violate everything that I think about the Christian gospel. The Christian gospel, to me, can be summed up in a trinitarian formula: God creates all people in God's image. God loves all people in Jesus Christ. God calls all people to the fullness of their humanity in the Holy Spirit. How you implement that formula is my mission and the mission of the church, as I see it.

What are you most proud of in your career in the church?

I think the thing I'm proudest of in my life is that I was a good father and a good husband. As a bishop there are two things that I'm proudest of. I'm proud of the fact that five of my clergy have been elected bishops in the

Episcopal Church, four have been elected cathedral deans, and another half dozen are serving in the largest parish in the diocese in which they live. So I think we've raised up an enormous amount of leadership within the Episcopal Church. In terms of ministry, I'm proudest of the fact that within this diocese we have broken the barriers that have precluded the involvement in the church of people of color, of women, and of gay and lesbian people. I'm proud that I have more than thirty gay and lesbian priests in my diocese. I'm proud that we had the first black dean of a cathedral in the United States. I'm proud that of my five largest churches, two of them have women rectors. I'm proud of the fact that in this diocese we had the first female archdeacon in the Anglican Communion. I'm proud that back in 1981 I ordained an Englishwoman as a priest because the church in England would not do that. I'm pleased with the fact that the countries of Uganda and Kenya both ordained women after their bishops visited this diocese and got to know some of our women clergy. I'm proud of all these things.

How important do you think it is to know what other religions believe?

I think that religious systems tend to move toward making excessive claims for their truth. Certainly Christianity has claimed that we have the whole truth of God. I think that's nonsense. I think the truth of God is beyond any religious system. I don't want to place myself in a position where I judge whether or not God is at work among Hindu people or Jewish people or Buddhist people. My experience is that God-intoxicated people are present within every religious tradition. They come into their God experience through their own pathways, and it's not up to me to tell God what pathway people can use to come to God. For me, the pathway is still through Jesus Christ. But that's because I am a child of the Western world and it's who I am. I'm not interested in giving that up. I *am* interested in claiming that my path is necessary for me, but I would never say that it's necessary for anybody else. That's God's business, not my business. We have a lot to learn from other faith traditions.

What advice do you have for a young person who might be searching for a path to follow?

Without meaning to quote Shakespeare instead of the Bible, I would say, "This above all: to thine own self be true, / And it must follow, as the night the day, / Thou canst not then be false to any man." Religion that forces you to deny who you are cannot be the truth of God. I would hope that any spiritual quest would be a quest not just into the reality of God, but into the reality of your own humanity. I see those as simultaneous quests. I think the more deeply you discover who you are, the more deeply you will discover who God is, because they are deeply related one to the other. So I would say find yourself, be yourself, and when you do, recognize that the source of your being is the transcendent reality that we call by the name of God.

FOR MORE INFORMATION

ON-LINE RESOURCES

Episcopalian.org
www.episcopalian.org

The Episcopal Church Home Page
www.dfms.org

Both of the Web sites listed above provide information about the activities of the Episcopal Church, including lists of Episcopal churches across the country, links to related sites, and current news of interest to those in the church.

BOOKS

Making Sense of the Episcopal Church: An Introduction to Its History, by Ken Clark (Moorehouse Publishing Company, 1997). This book traces the history of the Episcopal Church in America from colonial times through the 1960s.
Women Speak: On God, Congregations, and Change, by Joanna Bowen Gillespie (Trinity Press International, 1995).

Women have been particularly active in the Episcopal Church, and this collection features writings about how a range of women have found their place in church life.

A Brief History of the Episcopal Church, by David L. Holmes (Trinity Press International, 1993). A short history of the Episcopal Church, from its founding to modern times.

A Circle of Quiet, by Madeleine L'Engle (HarperSan-Francisco, 1986). Best known as a writer of books for young adults (*A Wrinkle in Time*), L'Engle has long been an active voice in the Episcopal Church. This book is the first in a trio of journals she kept about her life, and much of the material centers on her lifelong journey to better understand God and her own spirituality. The other books in the trilogy are *The Summer of the Great-Grandmother* and *The Irrational Season.*

Honest to God, by John A. T. Robinson (Westminster John Knox Press, 1963). This is the book that Bishop John Shelby Spong found so inspirational to his life and work in the Episcopal Church.

Rescuing the Bible from Fundamentalism: A Bishop Rethinks the Meaning of Scripture, by John Shelby Spong (HarperSan-Francisco, 1992). In this controversial and influential book Bishop Spong discusses what he sees as a misinterpretation of the Bible by Fundamentalist Christian groups, who have attempted to use the Scriptures to defend their conservative views.

Why Christianity Must Change or Die: A Bishop Speaks to Believers in Exile, by John Shelby Spong (HarperSan-Francisco, 1998). Bishop Spong wrote this book to speak to others who, like himself, feel alienated from their religious tradition. In it he calls for a reexamination of Christianity to make it a place where everyone can feel welcome.

Starhawk

Cofounder, the Reclaiming Witchcraft Tradition

"At the heart of the tradition of witchcraft is a deep, meaningful part that doesn't require any costumes or fancy tools to understand. It's really about the way we learn to deepen our awareness and to focus our minds to reach states of consciousness where we can feel connected to all of nature and to everything around us."

When they hear the word *witch*, many people immediately think of the popular Halloween figure of an old, ugly woman wearing a pointy hat and riding a broom. Some people even think that witches are completely made-up creations, and that no real witches exist.

But witches do exist, and their religion, witchcraft (also sometimes called Wicca or the Craft), is one that is growing in popularity. Although witchcraft has existed as a religion for thousands of years in various forms and in different parts of the world, in the last three decades it has taken on a newer, more modern form based partly on old beliefs and practices, and partly on new ways of seeing the world and the practice of witchcraft. In 1985 witchcraft was recognized as a religion by the federal government of the United States for legal purposes. Now priests and priestesses of witchcraft can perform legally binding marriage ceremonies, just as the clergy of other religions can, and the rights of witches to practice their religion are protected along with the rights of those who practice other religions.

What witchcraft is and isn't can be a matter of opinion. Just as there are different branches of Christianity, there are different branches of witchcraft, each with its own beliefs and ways of worshiping. There are no particular books or set of rules that are followed by all witches, and there is no single leader of the religion. Some witches form groups, called covens, with other witches, but many also practice their religion on their own.

It is easier to say what witchcraft *isn't.* Witches do not worship Satan or the devil (they don't believe in such a figure), nor do they participate in animal or human sacrifices, or any activity that could bring harm to others. In fact, the one universal law accepted by all true witches is the Wiccan Rede, which states: "And it harm none, do as you will." Similarly, most witches believe that whatever kind of energy they send out into the world through their practices will come back to them three times as strong, and for this reason negative practices are not encouraged.

In general, witchcraft can be defined as a pagan religion, meaning that it is a pre-Christian religion that does not have a belief in one supreme God. Instead, the beliefs and practices of witchcraft focus primarily on exploring an individual's relationship to the seasonal cycles of nature. Witches believe that by becoming more attuned to this connection, they can make positive changes in their own life and, as a result, in the larger world. To this end, most witches celebrate a seasonal schedule called the Wheel of the Year, which is made up of eight important days, called sabbats. These days are the variable dates of the spring and autumn equinoxes (Ostara and Mabon) and the summer and winter solstices (Litha and Yule), as well as the fixed days of Samhain (October 31), Imbolc (February 2), Beltane (May 1), and Lammas (August 1). In addition, many witches follow closely the twenty-eight-day cycle of the moon, and the full moons (called esbats) are particularly important to them.

Though no single deity is worshiped by all witches, the deities are an important part of the religion. Many witches see their primary deity as the Goddess, which is why witchcraft is sometimes referred to as the Religion of the Goddess. Many witches also recognize a God figure. Both the Goddess and the God appear in many different forms under different names, and which form a witch chooses to work with can depend on many things, including personal choice, the time of year (certain deities are associated with certain days or events), and the kind of practice being performed.

Where many religions focus on working to achieve a better life after death, witchcraft is concerned primarily with working to make the current life a positive one, both for the individual and for others. Because of their belief that Earth is the sacred, living manifestation of the Goddess, and because they believe that a person's soul is reincarnated again and again to live on Earth and celebrate its creation, many witches today are very involved in issues such as environmentalism and human rights.

Starhawk is one of the leading voices in the witchcraft community. Her 1979 book, *The Spiral Dance*, in which she outlined the meaning and purposes of witchcraft and the Goddess tradition, is considered the most influential work of the modern witchcraft movement. A peace activist and environmentalist, she is the cofounder of the Reclaiming tradition, a branch of witchcraft that emphasizes the importance of environmental awareness, community building, and the sanctity of human rights.

What are your definitions of witchcraft and paganism?

Paganism is an Earth-based spirituality that sees what is sacred in the processes of nature. Witchcraft, or

Wicca, is one branch of paganism that is centered on celebrating the processes of nature embodied or personified in the form of the Goddess of birth, growth, death, and regeneration.

When many people hear words like witchcraft *and* Goddess, *they have all kinds of ideas about what they mean. Do you find that many people have great misconceptions about what witchcraft is?*

They do, because there has been a very concerted effort over the last four or five hundred years to paint anything that was left of the Goddess tradition of the past as being evil or having to do with harming people. But in reality the witchcraft that my tradition practices has nothing to do with any of that. It has to do with understanding and honoring nature and the balance found in nature. It's about finding and understanding our place in the cycle of nature.

Where do you think the misunderstandings come from?

From years of people, especially religious leaders, trying to associate witchcraft with some kind of devil or black magic. There are many complex historical, social, and religious reasons behind the persecution of those involved with Goddess worship and witchcraft. In many instances it was simply a matter of competition between the newer, God-centered religions and the older,

Goddess-centered ones. By labeling witches and witch-craft as something evil, religious leaders tried to turn people away from those forms of religion so that they would accept the new ones.

A lot of books about witchcraft talk about the Burning Times. Can you describe what this was?

The Burning Times was a period in history, roughly from the late 1400s to the end of the 1600s, when great numbers of people were tortured and killed for suppos-edly practicing witchcraft. Many of them were burned to death, which is where the term "the Burning Times" comes from. There is a lot of debate about exactly how many people were killed, but it's generally accepted that the number is in the hundreds of thousands.

And were all these people actually witches?

Most of these people were not witches in any way. They were simply people who had been dragged into court and accused of being witches for various reasons. You could be accused of being a witch simply because someone didn't like you, or because someone wanted your property. If anyone accused you of being a witch, the Inquisition, the people behind the witch hunts, would take you and torture you until you confessed. There was no way to prove your innocence. So of course most people just confessed to being witches.

This period of history really brought out the worst side of human nature. Because anyone could accuse anyone else of practicing witchcraft, people used this as a way to get revenge on their neighbors or on people they didn't like for some reason. And because the torturers demanded the names of other supposed witches, many people simply gave the names of anyone they could think of. There are two villages we know of in Germany, where after the witch burners came through, there were no women left alive because they all named one another as witches and were killed. So this is a really terrible and often forgotten part of our history, but it lives on today in the fear that many people have about the word *witch*.

Many other religions still perceive witchcraft as something evil. Why do you think that is?

First, I think that many people today still don't understand that witchcraft is actually a religion. Second, there is a great deal of resistance to accepting nature-based religions and giving them the same weight as text-based religions. For example, the Supreme Court has ruled that nature-based religions do not have the right to protect their lands. They basically said that they would not give these kinds of spiritual traditions the same importance they give to religions that are based on books supposedly written down thousands of years ago. Part of the reason is that if they did, it would have enormous economic ramifications. For instance, they would have to stop mining uranium on Hopi sacred lands, or clear-cutting old-grove redwood forests in California. Many things that big business does, and makes enormous profits on, would have to stop, because nature-based religions place enormous sacred value in living places on the earth. Our belief is that preserving these places holds far greater importance than making a profit from them does.

Why do you think that many people see nature-based spirituality as being less important than what they perceive as more traditional religions?

I think this is a new idea for a lot of people. Most people are raised in religions where they are taught that religion is about having a set of beliefs and holding on to them, following a sacred book or a list of rules handed down to them. It's very hard for people to break away from that way of thinking.

Many people have the idea that you must be born into a particular religion. For example, if your parents are Catholic or Baptist, then you're Catholic or Baptist as well. But for the most part, people are not born into witchcraft. How did you come to it?

I think what you're saying was true twenty years ago. But now there *is* a generation of people who were born into Wiccan families and grew up in the tradition. And we'll see more and more of these people as the years go on and more people are raised as pagans.

As for myself, I came to witchcraft in college. I was raised Jewish and was very involved with that tradition. But as I got older—this was in the 1960s—there really wasn't much of a role for women in Judaism in terms of any leadership positions. This was before there were any women rabbis, and women were very much in the background of Judaism. I was doing an anthropology project on witches with a friend, and we met some people who were practicing the Old Religion of the Goddess, as they called it. They began to talk to us, and as they talked I realized that what they believed in were things that I believed in. They believed that nature was sacred and that sexuality was sacred. They believed that women could actually be leaders in religion. These were all things that I felt strongly about.

Was it hard for you to move away from Judaism and from what you'd been raised in?

I felt it was more like an extension of what I believed, not an abandonment of it. You can't just stop being Jewish. You *are* Jewish. It's much more than just a religion. It's an entire culture. So I saw witchcraft as an extension of that. And as I've gotten older I've found more and more ways in which I can find an earlier Goddess tradition that lies behind Judaism, and ways of integrating the traditions that I grew up with into the ones I've grown to practice and love as a witch.

Do you find that you often bring aspects of other spiritual traditions into your own practice?

I think we've learned over the last few years to be very cautious about simply incorporating elements of other people's traditions into our own, because not all people want their traditions used in that way. But I think that one of the great gifts of being alive at this time is that you can't help but be influenced by all the different spiritual traditions that are out there. We have access to so much information, and so many different teachings and directions and dimensions. I know in my own life that all of the insights and all of the teachings certainly affect what I do and the rituals that I create and the way that I view the Goddess.

Do you think that being involved with Wicca has allowed you to do that—to open up to exploring and accepting other ways of cele-brating and worshiping?

Wicca is, in a way, very eclectic. It teaches us that there are many different paths to truth, and that no one religion or one teacher can claim to have the only truth. There are many ways of seeing the same thing. It very much encourages us to respect other traditions, and in particular to learn from them what we can.

Many people see certain aspects of witchcraft—especially the rituals and spells and costumes—and think that's all Wicca is. How much do these things actually define witchcraft?

I think a lot of people can't see beyond the costumes and the spells. Those are certainly a part of witchcraft, and often a part that initially attracts a lot of people to Wicca. And that's because they're fun, especially the costumes! But those are the window dressing or the icing to what witchcraft really is underneath. At the heart of the tradition of witchcraft is a deep, meaningful part that doesn't require any costumes or fancy tools to understand. It's really about the way we learn to deepen our awareness and to focus our minds to reach states of consciousness where we can feel connected to all of nature and to everything around us. And that is a serious discipline that requires work and training and dedication. Sometimes the costumes and tools and things can help focus the mind, but they aren't the essence of it.

Magic is a word that is tied to any discussion of witchcraft, and for many people it is the most controversial aspect of the religion. What is magic to you?

I like the definition of magic that the writer Dion Fortune used. She said that magic is the art of changing consciousness at will. There are many different levels of consciousness available to us as human beings. We can, with practice and with discipline, learn to achieve these different states and move in and out of them at will. We learn that each kind of consciousness is useful for different things. Some are deeply pleasurable. Others are deeply informative. Some are simply restful. So we can think of magic, in a way, as a kind of applied psychology that allows us to reach these different levels of awareness.

Many people have seen movies like The Craft, *or watched television shows like* Sabrina, the Teenage Witch *and* Charmed, *and think that magic is about casting spells that make a person fall in love or be popular. Does magic really work that way?*

It certainly *can* work that way. Again, the power of the trained, focused human mind can achieve amazing things. This isn't a belief exclusive to witchcraft. Almost every culture in the world, except for the last few hundred years of secular Western culture, has acknowledged those powers and worked with them in some way. These powers are not unlimited, but they are there.

However, the real question is not whether these things can be done, but whether or not it's a good idea to do them. I don't think it's any wiser or more fulfilling to try to make someone fall in love with you than it is to pay the person to pretend to be in love with you. Love is only really satisfying when it's a free gift of a free will. Love spells are notorious in popular lore about witch-craft, and many, many people attempt them. Sometimes they work. Sometimes they don't. But even when they do, they usually end up causing all kinds of trouble.

An example of real magic would be using your trained mind to try to open up pathways that lead you to love, or that show you the obstacles in your life that are preventing you from finding the love you seek. There are ways to help yourself achieve these things, and they might involve doing some kind of spell work, but the real magic is changing yourself to let love into your life.

Witches have a belief that whatever you send out through magic returns to you three times over. So if you're sending out love in the real sense—sending out healing—then that brings love and trust back into your life. If you're sending out hatred or curses, or even manipulation, like trying to force someone to fall in love with you, then you'll attract those elements back into your life.

But so many books about witchcraft are filled with spells for things like love and money. Do you think these things are harmful?

People are always looking for ways to make their life better, particularly if it can be done easily. So many people buy these kinds of books thinking that they can say a few words and light a candle and everything will be better. But they don't understand what they really need to do, or what witchcraft is really about beneath the surface, and so for those people I think this kind of thing can certainly be harmful. Many people don't understand that to cast a spell that works means doing everything you need to do on a physical plane to create the conditions necessary to make your magic work. For example, if you want a job, you can't just cast a job spell and sit around waiting for it to work. You have to go out and look for a job. You have to write a résumé. You have to develop the skills you need to get the job you want. But you can do spell work to help you remove the blocks in yourself and in your surroundings that might be preventing you from getting those things done.

Can you give me an example of how you use magic in your own life?

I have certain things that I do every day as part of my own ritual practice. One of them is a practice called grounding. This is a meditation practice where you sit for a moment and simply feel your connection to the earth. You draw energy up from the earth and let it move throughout your body. I also try to spend some time every day out in nature, in a place where I can open myself up into a neutral, observing state where I can look at what is happening around me. I look at the birds and the plants and the animals and just observe them. I

Starhawk

feel my place among them. For me that's magic. It changes my consciousness, and my awareness, by opening me up to seeing what the things in the nonhuman world around me are doing.

I also do rituals for healing when someone is sick. I might get together with other witches and do a ritual where we lay hands on a sick person and encourage her body to heal itself. There are many kinds of magic.

Some people might look at those things and say, "Well, you're just meditating." Why is that a religion?

Meditating is an aspect of many religions. If you look at the origins of the word *religion*, it means "relinking" or "reconnecting." So practices that involve opening up and reconnecting with what's around us are religious practices.

But I was talking about those things in relation to working magic. Magic is not the only aspect of witchcraft, or even the biggest part of witchcraft. Witchcraft as a religion involves a world view, a theology, a cosmology, and a mythology—all of the things that every religion has—that teach us about our place in the world and how we are to live in it. There are holidays we celebrate and rituals we do to celebrate those holidays, which carry us through the cycle of the year.

Most religions have a central figure that is worshiped or vener-ated—such as God, Jesus, or Buddha—some central figure around which the religion is focused. Would you say that in witchcraft the Goddess is a similar figure?

Our Goddess is probably closer to what Native Americans talk about when they talk about the Great Spirit, or what Buddhists talk about when they talk about the mind. We don't see the Goddess as this over-whelming figure who sits above us and issues com-mands and rules that we must obey. She is more of a poetic personification of the processes of nature going on around us. She can be seen in many different aspects. For example, she can be seen as the Moon, which gets dark and waxes to fullness, and then wanes, becoming dark again but always renewing herself. Every month we see that process of rebirth and renewal. Or we see plants that grow and then die, becoming part of the earth so that new plants can grow. All of these things are going on around us all the time.

For many religions the point of being in them is so that at the end of your life you arrive somewhere or achieve something better than being human. For example, for Buddhists the ultimate goal is enlightenment. For Christians the hope is that after death you go to heaven to escape the trials of life on Earth. What is the point of witchcraft?

In witchcraft our life in this world as a human being *is* the goal and the reward. Our traditional teaching is that when we die, we come back again as another human being, living among the people we've known and loved before, and are able to know and love them again. This world is seen as the living body of the Goddess, and there's no greater reward than to be alive in it and to be intimate with it and connected to it.

How can you remain in contact with a loved one who has died if that person's soul has gone on to be reincarnated as someone else?

The way I see it is that each of us has what I call a deep self, and this self is truly part of the Goddess. We are all a part of her, and of this constant process of birth and life and death and rebirth. That deep self puts out different personalities, kind of like a jellyfish that has a lot of different tentacles. So each life is like one of those tentacles, and what it experiences feeds back into the body of the jellyfish. Everything you learn, everything you do, the ways you grow and develop, all feed back into the deep self. Those different tentacles appear and die and disappear. So when you connect, say, with your dead aunt Elsie, you're connecting with that core of her that exists beyond time and beyond space as the deep self. But it isn't with the precise personality she was when she was here as Aunt Elsie, who died in 1943 and liked to play the piano and always wore pink. It's with her as her deep self. Maybe some of that particular life Aunt Elsie had will be there, but so will all the other lives her deep self has experienced.

You mentioned earlier that witchcraft is deeply involved with being part of the world. I know that for many witches this means being involved politically, particularly when it comes to environmental and human rights issues. Why do you think that, as a witch, it's important to be involved with these issues?

For me, if we believe that nature is sacred, then we have an obligation to protect what is sacred, to prevent these incredibly beautiful aspects of the earth from being destroyed. You will find a large pagan presence in many of the groups working to protect the earth. For example, here in California there is a young woman named Julia Butterfly, who has been sitting in a redwood tree for most of the year to prevent the grove it grows in from being cut down by loggers. That comes from her deep spiritual connection to the land, her belief that no one has the right to destroy this beautiful part of what she sees as sacred land. That is the motivation to be willing to give up so much of your life energy and your own comfort to try to preserve and protect the land.

How does that extend to human rights?

There's a lot of pagan activity around all kinds of social justice issues and concerns. For me that comes down to understanding that this life is supposed to be our reward, is supposed to be a blessing and a gift and a celebration. And if it's not, then something has gone wrong and something needs to change. We are not supposed to be miserable and starving and suffering and oppressed. We're supposed to be living here free and happy and with reasonable abundance. So if the world isn't that way, it's up to us to make it that way.

If things are supposed to be a certain way and witches—or anyone—are working for them to be that way but they still don't change, then how do you explain that?

That's a question I ask myself a lot. When the Gulf War broke out, my husband and I were driving down the street and I said, "Wait a minute. Isn't this what we've spent our whole adult lives trying to prevent?" The answer I gave myself is that, first of all, in the Goddess tradition the Goddess is not omnipotent. She doesn't know everything. The Goddess needs human help to make the world a beautiful place. We are partners with her in that, so we have to hold our end up. We can't depend on her to do it all for us.

The other answer is that changes do happen, but they often happen slowly and take time. A seed needs time to ripen. So does change, especially when we might be working for change in one direction but there are other powerful forces working for things to remain the same or to go in a different direction. All of these things balance each other out. Sometimes they work together, and sometimes they cancel each other out. All we can do is keep working for the changes we want to see come about.

I know I've seen tremendous changes in my lifetime. But with every political struggle I've ever been involved in, we never felt like we were winning at the time. Even when I can look back years later and see that we *were* winning it, at the time it didn't seem that way. So I think that one of the biggest lessons we have to learn is about being willing to keep on doing what we need to do, whether or not we're seeing immediate results from it.

Personally you have been extremely instrumental in bringing the Goddess tradition back to life in this country, particularly with your book The Spiral Dance. *It's now been twenty years since that book came out. When you look back on those years, how do you see your own connection to witchcraft having changed?*

There are things that have changed dramatically. The Craft has grown enormously in the last twenty years. But people continue to use that book as an introduction to witchcraft, and the basic stuff that I wrote in that book is the stuff that I still live by to this day. I know a lot more now than I did when I wrote that book. I know a tremendous amount now about magic and ritual and working with energy. But what I have learned all comes from the core beliefs I wrote about then.

Twenty years ago becoming a witch meant being a rebel and standing well outside of the mainstream. But now we've grown up, and the Craft has grown up as well. I think there is more of a sense now that we are as much a legitimate religion and tradition as any other, and that should be recognized. We should have the right to proclaim who we are and to raise our children and have them be able to go to school and talk about what they believe without fearing that someone will freak out and take them away from us.

Have you had moments of doubt over the years about whether or not what you believe is real?

I was in Israel earlier this year, where I've been several times. It's a wonderful place to go and be able to connect with the land and the ancestors and the energies of the people there. But when you're in Israel, you're also faced with some of the most die-hard fanatics of at least three of the world's major religions. As I looked around at these different groups I suddenly thought, "If this can happen to these religions, what's to stop it from happening to the Goddess religion?" And then the very next thought was, "Maybe I would have done better to have gone into marine biology instead of witchcraft."

But at the heart of it the Goddess religion is not so

much about belief. It's not about accepting that there is this external presence that I have to believe in. It's about really deeply understanding what is going on around us. So I might go back and forth about things like whether I really believe in the faeries and that they exist all around us. But I've never had doubts about the Goddess, because she is the process of life and death, and all I have to do is walk out my door and look at the leaves falling and decaying into the earth, and I know that process is what I worship in the form of the Goddess.

Some Christians will say that they feel "the still small voice" of God in their heart, and that's how they know he is with them. Do you feel a similar connection to the Goddess?

There are times when I feel that way about the Goddess, and there are times when it's more clear to me that the processes of nature are going on around me but that they aren't saying something to me specifically. I've always pretty much followed my own inner voice, which tells me what is right for me and what is the right way to go. And there is a kind of gut-level feeling to that, which I have learned to trust deeply. In any religion, or in any tradition, we are better off with cultivating a certain amount of healthy skepticism, because if you look at history, the worst wrongs have been done by people who were deeply sure that they were right.

Starhawk   139

In the Goddess tradition we believe that we have the right to argue with the Goddess. The Goddess has many aspects, and there are Gods as well as Goddesses. If one of those aspects tells you something, you have the right to go and get a second opinion, as it were. And if one of them tells you something that goes against your own common sense or your own sense of right and wrong, you have a right to say no.

What has been the most positive aspect of being a part of the Wiccan community for you?

It's not something that has added to my life; it is something that has completely shaped my life. I feel very fortunate that the work that I do, the relationships that I have, the community that I am a part of, are able to be integrated so tightly. I feel very lucky to be surrounded by people who aren't perfect but are trying to work toward the same sense of connectedness with the earth that I am. I am thankful that I have been able to go to many of the beautiful, magical places on the earth, and that I can live in one such place. I have a daily connection with the life processes going on around me, and that's wonderful.

What have been some of the hardest things for you to deal with?

The hardest thing about being a witch is the general misunderstanding there is about witchcraft, and the prejudice that people have against it. I feel that part of my work in the world is to confront that and to educate people about what witchcraft is and isn't, and that takes up an enormous amount of energy.

What do you see as the biggest challenge for witchcraft as a religion in the coming years?

One of our challenges now is to find ways to grow and develop without losing some of the incredible excitement and creativity that was what fueled us twenty years ago when this modern revival started. We need to bring new people into a tradition where there is now a real body of knowledge and training, but retain the same sense of empowerment we felt when we originally created the rituals and were forming the tradition we have. We have to pass all this on to our children, to the next generation. Witchcraft is often called the Old Religion, but in many ways I think it's more the New Religion. If you look at the actual stuff we do and practice, very little of that has really come down to us through the ages. It's evolved and been distilled out of what we are dealing with today and our response to it. And for me that's what keeps it alive and exciting. We don't simply have to say the same words that someone has been saying for thousands of years. We have to look at the words we say and see why they have meaning to us now. That way, when we create songs or chants or rituals, they have power because they come from within ourselves, and not from some old book or from what someone else has said before us.

FOR MORE INFORMATION

ON-LINE RESOURCES

With the increasing interest in witchcraft and related topics, there are thousands of Web sites devoted to these subjects. But not all of them are good. Many contain misleading and even false information, and some are just plain ridiculous. If you are interested in finding accurate, truthful information about witchcraft or paganism, start with some of the sites listed below. They contain links to other quality sites with reliable information.

The Witches' Voice
www.witchvox.com

The Witches' Voice is an organization devoted to providing news of interest to the witch community, and fair and accurate information about witches and their beliefs. Its extensive Web site is one of the most valuable resources for those seeking up-to-date information about the goings-on in the community. Not only does it cover current events, but it also contains essays and articles about a variety of topics related to witches and witch-craft, as well as hundreds of links to other quality sites.

The Witches' League for Public Awareness
www.celticcrow.com

WLPA is an educational network dedicated to correcting misinformation about witches and witchcraft. Its Web site provides information for people fighting discrimination against witches and contains substantial information about the rights of witches to practice their religion freely.

Reclaiming
www.reclaiming.org

Reclaiming is the organization that Starhawk cofounded. Located in San Francisco, it offers classes and public rituals for those interested in learning more about witchcraft and celebrating the different holidays. Its Web site also contains information about other pagan and witch groups.

BOOKS

Just as there are a lot of Web sites passing off silly ideas as real witchcraft, there are a lot of inaccurate books about the religion. The books that follow, however, are all excellent sources of information.

Wicca: The Old Religion in the New Millennium, by Vivianne Crowley (Thorsons, 1996). Crowley, who has a doctorate in psychology, is a leading figure in Western paganism. Her book clearly sets forth the principles of witchcraft and provides an excellent foundation for further study or research.

Wicca: A Guide for the Solitary Practitioner (Llewellyn Publications, 1988) and *Living Wicca: A Further Guide for the Solitary Practitioner* (Llewellyn Publications, 1993), both by Scott Cunningham. Cunningham is the foremost author of do-it-yourself books on witchcraft, and these two books are good introductions to almost everything you need to know about what witches are and what they do.

Book of Shadows: A Modern Woman's Journey into the Wisdom of Witchcraft and the Magic of the Goddess, by Phyllis Curott (Broadway Books, 1998). Curott is an Ivy League–educated attorney and witch. This autobiography details how she came to study witchcraft and discusses the challenges she has faced reconciling her religion with her position in the corporate world.

The Witches' Goddess (Phoenix Publishing, 1987) and *The Witches' God* (Phoenix Publishing, 1989), both by Janet and Stewart Farrar. The Farrars have written extensively on a variety of topics related to witchcraft. In these two books they present a wealth of information about how the Goddess and the God are seen in witchcraft, and the various forms each takes.

People of the Earth: The New Pagans Speak Out, by Ellen Evert Hopman and Lawrence Bond (Destiny Books, 1996). This is an extensive collection of interviews with pagans and witches from many different traditions. Most of the influential figures from the pagan and witch communities are included, and their candid interviews provide unique insight into what it means to be involved in these spiritual traditions.

21st-Century Wicca: A Young Witch's Guide to Living the Magical Life, by Jennifer Hunter (Citadel Press, 1998). This practical, engaging book by a young witch is perfect for those who want to know what it means to be a witch in today's world. Hunter packs a lot of information into this book, which includes a section devoted to the challenges of practicing witchcraft while still in high school or college.

The Spiral Dance, by Starhawk (HarperCollins, 1979). This is one of the most influential of all the books written about modern witchcraft and Goddess worship. It contains information about witchcraft, as well as many different meditations and rituals designed to further understanding of basic principles of witchcraft.

The Reverend
Dr. J. Philip Wogaman
President, the Interfaith Alliance

"There is no Christian answer to anything that comes out of an unloving foundation. If what you're hearing seems to be motivated by hate and divisiveness, then it probably isn't truly Christian, or Jewish or Muslim or Buddhist or whatever your faith is. The foundation of right, the foundation of good, is always love."

Christianity is the dominant religion of the world, with approximately one-third of the population belonging to one Christian church or another. But trying to define all Christian churches the same way is an impossible task, as each church that calls itself "Christian" has differing beliefs and practices. For example, Baptists and Catholics are both Christian groups, but they have very different sets of beliefs and ways of worshiping.

In general, Christianity is a religion that follows the

146

teachings of and about Jesus Christ of Nazareth. Jesus was a Jewish teacher who lived approximately two thousand years ago and who was executed by the Roman authorities for his beliefs and actions around the year A.D. 30.

Apart from this commitment to following the teachings of Jesus as collected in the books of the Bible, the different Christian groups frequently have little in common. Most Christians regard Jesus as the Son of God sent to Earth to teach humankind how to live, and many believe that because of his death and subsequent resurrection three days later, he paid the debt for mankind's sins, and those who believe in him will be saved from eternal damnation after death. But not all do. Some see Jesus as a man who achieved a godlike nature through devotion and good works, and believe that all people can achieve the same status.

There are currently about twelve hundred formal Christian organizations in North America. Divisions between some of these groups can be very wide, and frequently different Christian groups come into conflict with one another, and with other religions, over disagreements of belief. The Interfaith Alliance is an organization founded to bring people of different religious backgrounds together in an attempt to understand one another's views and to support one another's right to religious freedom of expression. It also acts as a political organization, challenging the views of ultraconservative

Christian organizations and other conservative groups that attempt to influence public policy in the United States.

Dr. J. Philip Wogaman is a Methodist minister and the current president of the Interfaith Alliance. He has been a professor of Christian ethics at Wesley Theological Seminary, president of the Society of Christian Ethics in the United States and Canada, and dean of Wesley Seminary. He is the author of more than a dozen books and was a member of the World Methodist Council. In addition to his work with the Interfaith Alliance he is the pastor of Foundry United Methodist Church in Washington, D.C., which has gained public recognition as the church attended by President Bill Clinton and First Lady Hillary Rodham Clinton.

What was your view of religion and spirituality when you were a teenager?

A fair amount of my interest in religion was generated in those years by religious-camp experiences. I grew up in a religious home. My father was a Methodist minister. So I never knew a time when religion wasn't front and center, even well before there was any degree of spiritual content in my own thoughts. It was always an essential aspect of our life as a family. But I think those youth camps I attended were very important to my personal development. It was a challenging time, and we were encouraged to pray alone under the trees. I had some fairly intense moments of prayer there, and I remember carrying a lot of that back with me to my everyday life.

A lot of people speak about developing faith as young people because they were afraid of dying or afraid of what would happen to them. Do you remember what attracted you to faith at that age?

I don't think it had anything to do with fear. Maybe at certain points I would feel guilt, but I don't remember being afraid. My father didn't believe in or teach about a literal hell, so that wasn't a factor for me. I don't remember it ever being stressed or believed in most of the circles that I was involved in.

Because of the home I grew up in, faith became routine. It was just always there. When I came to a point of making a conscious decision about my faith, in my teen years, it was due to the freshness of a spiritual appeal that came in from outside the family. That wasn't a rejection of my family, but something from outside my immediate family made me decide to take a fresh look at what it all meant to me.

What was that influence?

In my high school years, as I reflected on what I might want my lifework to be, I was attracted by four possibilities. One of them was ministry. That was always there as an option. One was law. One was teaching high school. And one was music. I was a pretty good pianist, and I think I could have made a serious career of music. Those options kind of vaguely floated around in my mind, and I thought about one or another of them at different times.

I can almost name the time and the place when it crystalized in the direction of ministry, however, and that was in the early summer of 1950. I had just finished high school, and I was at one of those youth camps I mentioned before. There was a particularly appealing young preacher who spoke very convincingly about the calling to ordained ministry. I don't remember specifically anything he said, but his overall message stayed with me.

It had nothing to do with the fact that your father was a minister?

In an odd kind of way I felt in my bones that I could not follow a calling just because it was my father's calling. The idea of ministry had always been a tantalizing possibility, but it was in that week of June in 1950 that the idea became a firm decision. I would say in retrospect that it was a pretty immature decision. It wasn't based on anything profound, and it wasn't terribly well thought out. But it was heartfelt. And like many decisions we make and things that really shape us, it set a foundation from which real growth was possible. I never had to turn

Paths of Faith

back from it. The particular direction that my ministry has taken over the years has been subject to considerable variation, but the decision to pursue ordination was kind of set in place at that moment.

When you are pastoring a church, how different do you find the experience of being a religious leader from being responsible only for your own spirituality?

Most of my ministry—thirty-one years of it—has been spent in teaching at various academic institutions. I have spent eight in pastoral ministry. For every Christian, in addition to one's own faith experience, there is one's interaction with other people who are being influenced by you. Leadership in that spiritual sense is not restricted to clergy or ordained pastors. It's more intensely focused there, and even institutionalized through preaching and pastoral counseling. The things that a pastor routinely does involve leadership roles. But that's not restricted to a pastor. Leadership comes in a slightly different form in the pastoral role than it does in the teaching role, but you influence people in both positions.

Do different things appeal to you about teaching than appeal to you about pastoring?

There are differences, but I would not want to exaggerate them. In the pulpit one is teaching as well as inspiring. And in the classroom one is inspiring as well as teaching. That is, in the classroom, particularly if you are teaching ethics, you're dealing with values. You're attempting to persuade, as well as to illuminate, and help people see the options. In the pulpit, as you preach, you're appealing to the faith and reinforcing the faith. You're reinforcing our capacity to love and to care for one another. But you are also teaching. You're helping people grapple with the intellectual issues they might have as they contemplate their own faith. I wouldn't want to overstate the differences, but they are two different things. The rhythm of life is different. When I preach, I have to prepare a new sermon for almost every Sunday. During the week I have pastoral contacts to make. As one of my colleagues remarked, the exciting thing for him about ministry is that every day is unique and different. There's some truth to that.

How do you find pastoring affects your own spiritual journey?

I have felt deeply challenged to grow. I think the process of preparing to preach has been, for me, a wonderful opportunity to focus my own growth.

How did you come to be involved in the Interfaith Alliance?

That was in the fall of 1994. I was among many people in our country who were and are deeply concerned about religious extremism as exemplified particularly by the Christian Coalition and groups of that sort. I felt there was need for a voice in our country that would challenge the assumptions of the religious extremists and help people see a broader and more mature way to express their faith in public life. Along came the Interfaith Alliance. I was not one of the founders, but I joined the board in 1994, about six months after the organization was founded. I was excited by the prospect of a national organization that would explicitly embrace the whole spectrum of American religions. I feel that there is much need for that, and quite apart from the public policy or political side of the alliance's work, this is a vehicle for interreligious dialogue and cooperation. I think that's very important.

Why do you think that kind of dialogue is important?

I think interacting with different religions and learning about other people's spiritual beliefs can only help you learn more about your own. It also gives me a greater sense of the richness of all the religious traditions. In 1967 I published a book called *Protestant Faith and Religious Liberty*. It was during a period when there had been a lot of national discussion of religious-liberty questions. In writing that book I took great intellectual inspiration from philosopher Paul Tillich's principle of criticizing all earthly absolutes, and from the notion that

The Reverend Dr. J. Philip Wogaman   153

God is greater than any of us. Therefore, as we approach people of other faiths it should be our expectation that we will find something of God in them that we should attend to. I find that a profound source of support for the concept of religious liberty.

Now that I am interacting with people of different religions on a regular basis and much more deeply, that idea keeps coming home to me. It's not that I have all of the truth and that people of other religions are in error and I simply tolerate them so that we can all get along. It's that there's something positive and rich in what we are *all* doing as individual faiths that is worth sharing. That doesn't mean that I am in any way turning my back on the central aspects of my own faith. I think it helps to illuminate the meaning of God's love more deeply.

What about when it comes to aspects of other religions that you might disagree with?

If God is greater than any of us, it means that we are all prone to error and to mistakes. We need to be aware of those mistakes. For instance, I'm not hesitant in saying that religious traditions that put women in a second-class position are wrong. I think they are wrong, and I think they're hurting themselves. That's true of an awful lot of religions in the world today, and it needs to be addressed. But I am confident that with time those people who do such things will see that it isn't the right thing to

Paths of Faith

do. Most of us can take criticism if we feel that the critic loves us more than the critic hates whatever it is she or he is criticizing.

Do you think that most faiths are looking for the same thing underneath all the differences?

I'm not sure. I suppose you could say that on an unconscious level every faith is looking toward a sense of assurance that we're at home in this universe, that our lives matter, and that we have a basis of fellowship with others on the same journey. But there are many variations of religion, and some of them are extremely narrow. I'm not always sure that I'm really looking for the same thing that an extreme Fundamentalist is looking for, for example. There's a negative influence acting there. I will say that in interactions with Fundamentalists, I've found it possible sometimes to get beneath the surface of our disagreements to talk about God's grace and to make a connection with them. But it's hard.

When you look at an organization like the Christian Coalition, and at their very negative tactics and attempts to influence politics, does it anger you that they imply that they speak for all Christians?

At the very least it annoys me. But I think sadness is my greatest feeling. Apart from my work with the Interfaith Alliance, the fact that I am the pastor of a

The Reverend Dr. J. Philip Wogaman   155

church attended by President Clinton—who has often been the target of attacks by the Religious Right—means that sometimes I am directly in the middle of the firestorm. I've gotten a fair amount of hate mail, and every so often there will be a demonstration in front of the church. I find people who are involved in those things are, on the whole, pretty fearful people. Somehow I want to cut through all of the differences to find out why they're hurting so badly.

Have you been able to do that?

Sometimes you can. One day there was a demonstration out in front of the church. It was sponsored by Operation Rescue, or one of those antiabortion groups. It was bitterly cold, so we had our minister of missions and some of the laypeople go out and bring them hot chocolate and doughnuts. They told them that we loved them and wanted them to know we weren't upset with them.

How did that go over?

They had to ask their leader whether or not it was okay to eat the doughnuts, but after that it was fine. We invited them inside, but they didn't take us up on that.

As you mentioned, your church has been thrust into a political spotlight because President Clinton attends. How do you deal with the fact that what should be a very personal subject—spirituality—is suddenly a political issue?

It's very difficult. Religious faith proclaimed in public by a political figure can easily become the basis for cynicism. People are very quick to say that he's only doing it for political reasons. But the other side of that is that if a public figure is entirely private about religious faith, he becomes accused of not being religious enough. For the leader there is a dilemma there, and I respect that.

How do you offer spiritual advice to someone in his position?

In ministering to people in such a setting it helps to be able to reinforce the idea that a public life is in many ways itself a religious vocation. And it helps to offer the kind of support that religious faith can provide in making a person a more whole person and in helping someone to remember that the stereotypes that appear in public are not who you really are.

I think it also helps public figures to see that in the long run of eternity our positive accomplishments will add up to something, but our reputation and public image itself will fade, no matter who you are, even if you're the president of the United States. A million years from now, and even much sooner than that, no one will really remember what people thought about any of us. But the good things that we do will, hopefully, live on. We're like

The Reverend Dr. J. Philip Wogaman   157

sand castles on the beach. A wave comes along and wipes us away. But what we accomplish remains.

Do you think that religious groups and religious issues have too big a part in politics?

I think one's religious faith ought to inform everything that one does. If one's religious faith is narrow, then the effect of that in the public sphere will be destructive. But if one's religious faith is humble and loving, the effect of that in the public sphere will be to reinforce the most positive values of the community, and that makes a big difference. I don't think the answer to the narrow is to compartmentalize one's life. Of course, the government as such is probably neutral, and on that I think our First Amendment tradition is sound. But for a public figure, and for those of us who are citizens who act politically through our voting and through our advocacy, the big line of demarcation is between a narrow and sometimes vindictive view of life and one that is more humble and loving.

More and more, especially with the impeachment hearings of President Clinton that occurred in 1999, we see morality being pushed into political life. Do you think that's appropriate?

It has always been part of public life. Remember, when President Kennedy was elected, it was a big deal that he was the first Catholic president. And it was a

Paths of Faith

transforming event in regard to how Catholicism was seen in public life. Certainly with the Clinton investigation various moral issues have been used politically. I think the country is in a struggle to define its soul. There will be no simple definition, but it really is a contrast between a view of our society that is spiritually deep and concerned with growth in fellow feeling and love and all of those virtues, and a view that is narrow, legalistic, fearful, and condemnatory.

What is your advice to people who might have been taught by their faith that certain things are absolutely right or wrong, and now are having questions about what they've been taught?

You have to apply the test of love. There is no Christian answer to anything that comes out of an unloving foundation. If what you're hearing seems to be motivated by hate and divisiveness, then it probably isn't truly Christian, or Jewish or Muslim or Buddhist or whatever your faith is. The foundation of right, the foundation of good, is always love. That's the test. Obviously there's much more to it than that, but if you don't start at that point, you can't go any further. Most of the moral rules that we live by get their strength from that. And we must have moral rules and abide by them, but the ultimate test is love.

Has your view of how God operates in the world changed through all of the different things you've been involved in during your life?

The Reverend Dr. J. Philip Wogaman 159

I don't believe that God is manipulating our lives as if we were only puppets. I suppose the longer you live, the more you're aware of how tragic evil is in the world, and at the same time how goodness can spring forth when you're least expecting it and take you by surprise. The first great struggle in my adult life was the civil rights struggle. I was born into a world with racial segregation and with the evil repression of people based solely on the color of their skin. It seemed at the time that it could never change. But then along came the civil rights movement, and a lot of other things, and it was as though God's spirit were suddenly bursting forth. It created change that we thought might not be possible.

Can you think of a time when your own faith led you to speak out like that?

My first experience, personally, with publicly witnessing to the implications of my religious faith occurred when I was about thirteen. I had a seventh-grade teacher who was deeply racist. She believed that African American people were inferior. She was anti-Semitic. She was just very, very narrow and prejudiced. She used to pepper her discussions in the classroom with anecdotes and stories to illustrate the inferiority of other people. That was the opposite of what I was learning at home and of what I believed. Finally one day I had had enough of it. She made a racist statement, and I stood up in my seat and said, "That's not so."

She was deeply offended by that. My mother was teaching in the same school, and my teacher accosted her on the playground during recess and demanded to know what she was going to do about my outburst. My parents were slightly embarrassed but very, very proud. I think it says more about the background I came from than it does about any strength of character on my part, but it's an example of how your faith can influence you to action.

What, for you, is the point of a life spent in faith?

It's what a real life is. Everything else is settling for something less than real life. It's a life in harmony with God, who is the one who has given us the gift of life and gives us the promise of eternal life. That's much more than getting to go to heaven when you die. It's being part of God's eternal goodness. And it all begins right here.

FOR MORE INFORMATION

ON-LINE RESOURCES

The Interfaith Alliance
www.tialliance.org

The Web site for the Interfaith Alliance provides information about TIA activities, discusses current events relating to the religious community, and offers extensive links to Web sites about many other religions and religious organizations, both those TIA supports and those it opposes. By starting here, you can learn a great deal about both sides of the issues currently being debated by churches, and about the role religion is playing in national and world affairs.

BOOKS

Trying to pick only a few books about Christianity out of the thousands available is nearly impossible. Because this book is about how people experience spirituality, the list below features books that deal with the issue of people exploring their place in the Christian Church.

Confessions: The Making of a Post-denominational Priest, by Matthew Fox (HarperSanFrancisco, 1997). Fox is a former Dominican priest and a very controversial figure in the church. His autobiography is a fascinating example of what happens when a person's faith is challenged by his experiences.

Rattling Those Dry Bones: Women Changing the Church, by June Steffensen Hagen (Lura Media, 1995). The twenty-three essays in this collection were written by women who have worked to transform the various Christian churches they belong to.

Christianity and Culture in the Crossfire, by David A. Hoekema and Bobby Fong (William B. Eerdmans, 1997). This collection of essays, written by leading voices in Christian philosophy and ethics, examines some of the social and political issues that the Christian Church faces today.

Finding Our Voices: Women, Wisdom, and Faith, by Patricia O'Connell Killen (Crossroad Publishing, 1997). Another excellent book about the role of women in the church.

Mere Christianity, by C. S. Lewis (Touchstone Books, 1993). C. S. Lewis is best known as the author of the Chronicles of Narnia series of children's books, but he was also one of Christianity's greatest thinkers and writers. This book is based on a series of radio lectures Lewis gave in 1943, addressing what he considered the central issues of Christianity.

The Global God: Multicultural Evangelical Views of God, by Aida Besancon Spencer and William David Spencer (Baker Book House, 1998). A collection of essays written by people from many different ethnic groups about how their particular culture views God.

From the Eye of the Storm: A Pastor to the President Speaks Out, by J. Philip Wogaman (Geneva Press, 1999).

Written by Rev. Wogaman during the national debate over the impeachment trial of President Bill Clinton, this book provides a fascinating look at how the president's pastor viewed the situation.

Dr. Uma Mysorekar

President, the Hindu Temple Society
of North America

*"When I come to the temple and I look at the deities
and stand in the moment, I feel a tremendous unloading of my burdens and a great inner peace. I am
experiencing that. It is not just in my mind."*

The word *Hindu* is derived from the Persian word for
Indian, and reflects the fact that Hinduism has its roots
in the civilizations that lived in the Indus River valley
region from 4000 to 2200 B.C. The religion was later
influenced by the beliefs of different groups that
invaded the region, particularly peoples from Russia and
central Asia, whose beliefs mixed with the indigenous
Indian beliefs.

Hinduism differs from Christianity and other
Western religions in that it does not have a single
founder, a specific theological system, a single set of
moral laws, or any defined organizational structure.

165

Central to Hindu beliefs are several sacred texts, the most important of which is the Bhagavad Gita, a poem describing a conversation between the warrior Arjuna and his charioteer, Krishna. Another important text is the Rig-Veda, a collection of more than a thousand hymns. Other texts include the Brahmanas, the Sutras, and the Aranyakas.

At the heart of Hinduism is the idea that the entire universe is one divine entity who is simultaneously at one with the universe and transcends it. God is visualized as a trinity comprised of Brahma, the creator, who is continuing to create new realities; Vishnu (Krishna), the preserver, who preserves these new creations; and Siva, the destroyer, who is alternately compassionate and destructive. Most Hindus follow one of two major divisions within Hinduism: Vaishnavism, which generally regards Vishnu as the ultimate deity, and Shivaism, which generally regards Siva as the ultimate deity. In addition many hundreds of Hindu gods and goddesses are worshiped as various aspects of the divine trinity.

In Hinduism humans are perceived as being trapped in a cycle of birth, life, death, and rebirth. Karma is the accumulated sum of a person's good and bad deeds, and determines how that person will be reincarnated to live his or her next life. Hindus believe that through pure acts, thoughts, and devotion one can be reborn at a higher level, and eventually one can escape the cycle of reincarnation and achieve enlightenment. But if one lives a bad or immoral life, one may be reincarnated at a lower level in order to learn the lessons not learned in the previous lifetime.

Hinduism is the world's third-largest religion, practiced by about 13 percent of the world's population. About 80 percent of Hindus are Vaishnavas. Others follow various reform movements or neo-Hindu sects. Hinduism has a deserved reputation of being highly tolerant of other religions. This is summed up in the Hindu saying *"Ekam Sataha Vipraha Bahudha Vadanti,"* which may be translated, "The truth is One, but different Sages call it by Different Names."

Dr. Uma Mysorekar is president of the Hindu Temple Society of North America, an organization that links Hindu temples across the United States and Canada, promotes Hindu worship, and educates the public about Hindu beliefs and practices. She is also a medical doctor.

What were your earliest experiences with Hindu faith?

My experience in Hindu faith is actually the experience of my life. I don't know of any other faith. I was born into this, I was indoctrinated into it, I grew up in it, and I will die in it. This does not mean that I have not learned about other religions, which I have always done and continue to do. But my day-to-day life is surrounded by the teachings of Hinduism.

Did you ever have moments when you separated religious beliefs from the rest of your life?

It was always very much closely connected. I was born in India and raised in a family that was a very religious one. My family, like many others in India and elsewhere, started each morning with prayers before we went about our business. We would pray again in the evening when we came home, before we ate dinner, and again before we went to bed. Now, how much time one spends in prayer depends upon both the available time and one's own choices. I don't think that should be the measure of anyone's belief or faith. But for many of us, when we start the morning with prayer, then whatever the day may hold and however difficult it may appear, it seems as if we have the strength of our spirituality and our faith behind us. Somehow it eases any difficulties we may encounter.

Why do you think prayer is so effective?

Somebody recently asked me, "Don't you think this is all in your mind?" And the answer is no, it is not all in my mind. When I come to the temple and I look at the deities and stand in the moment, I feel a tremendous unloading of my burdens and a great inner peace. I am experiencing that. It is not just in my mind. And I am not alone in this. There are millions of people for whom prayer and contemplation are very real events. I think religion should be a part of everyone's life, no matter what their beliefs are. This whole notion of going to Sunday school or just going to religious places on Sundays alone—in my opinion that is not correct. God doesn't take holidays. He is there with us at all times. In fact, almost every religion agrees on one thing: God, or whatever you call that power, is within us. So if God is always within us, how can we say that we serve God only on Sunday or Saturday or whatever day we choose? He or she—the Supreme Power—lives within us. That is why Hindu teachings tell us that we must respect ourselves and we must respect others. If you firmly believe that God is within you, then respect is going to come naturally. Older people. Younger people. It doesn't matter. When you accept that God is within you and within others, and you respect yourself and others because of that, then you have accomplished a great deal.

Did you ever feel, or do you ever feel, like the prayers are a burden and you don't want to do them?

I never felt they were a burden. But of course there were occasions when my mother would say, "You must do all of these things today. Finish your prayers before you go." And if there was pressure to finish my chores, or later to do my work in college, then I might wish I didn't have to do them. But in the evening, when I came

Dr. Uma Mysorekar   169

home, I used to tell my mother that this was how I felt. I was glad that I could say those things to her. She never got angry. She sat me down and explained to me, "I ask you to do this not so that by taking an extra ten minutes to pray you feel great, but to teach you a form of discipline." If you know that a particular day is a special day and you need to do special prayers, you will know to plan an extra ten minutes into your day to do that. That is the discipline I learned.

How did you feel about the gods themselves and their role in your life?

When I was young, we only looked at gods where they were placed. In every Hindu home there is a room that is designated for worship. Different images of deities and special holy books are kept there. Services are done only in that particular room, and it is a very holy place. Temples are also holy places. So when I was young, I thought of the gods as existing in those special places or temples. But as I grew up I realized that God was not in only those places. He was in every single place you could go. It doesn't really matter where I go to worship. I can sit in a car. I can sit in a yard. I can sit in a park. I can sit anyplace and I can still reach the Supreme Power, just by concentrating and not thinking about anything else. And when I do that, I do speak to God. This happened, of course, much later in life. Earlier on, as most kids will do, I would go to that special room or to the temple and say my prayers the way my parents taught me to. But it was not the same experience as it was later.

When did it change for you?

When I was in medical school. That's when I realized that worship was much more than just looking at images and saying some words. Then I came to the United States, where I have had the pleasure of meeting people from many different cultures and religious backgrounds. That helped me to see that almost all of us have the same basic goals in our worship. Unfortunately, we don't implement them the same way, and that causes confusion. We fight about it.

The Hindu gods have always seemed very accessible to me, as they are portrayed as being very human in many ways. Did you feel that way when you were growing up?

Absolutely. When I was distressed, I would go someplace and I would put an image of Lord Ganesha in front of me. I would meditate on it and ask him to help me. I would say my prayers to him and ask for guidance. And every time, either that evening or by the next day, I would receive an answer. Now, it's possible that when we pray so intently, God gives us that power back to resolve the problem ourselves. In other words, he works through us. He may give us the problem in the first place, but he also gives us the power to work through it by ourselves. Lord Ganesha, in particular, is known for creating problems in order to solve problems. He happens to be the Hindu god with whom I have the greatest rapport, so he is very special to me.

You call Ganesha a god, but you also talk about a God as if there is just one. Can you explain that?

In Hinduism there are different forms of God: one who creates, one who protects, and one who destroys. These are the three principles of life. The one who creates is Brahma. The one who protects is Vishnu. The one who destroys is Siva. These are the eternal trinity principles. All the other deities are the different forms of God. But ultimately God is one.

So each god or goddess is a different aspect of the one God, and you choose the aspect that appeals to you most?

For example, if I meet you today, I might take a liking to you. I might like the way that you speak to me and the way that you present yourself. But I might then meet someone else whom I don't like, for whatever reason. The same thing happens with the deities. For some reason—and I don't know what it is—many of us develop a special feeling toward a particular deity. We are able to see our problems and our experiences in those of that deity. We have confidence that this deity will listen to us and help us.

How important do you think it is for people to develop that kind of a relationship with a supreme power?

I think that whatever form of religion they follow, it is important for young people to understand that they must make spirituality a part of their lives. Without spirituality life becomes incomplete. Just like your daily ritual— getting up, taking a shower, getting dressed, eating breakfast—spirituality should also be a natural part of every day. Because ultimately we have to ask ourselves the question, Who is it that created us, and why are we here? There are two things that are certain in this world. One is life, and the other is death. Therefore, who determines who is born? Who determines who dies? There must be some supreme power. It doesn't matter who it is, but it is important that we try to relate to it. In order for us to live a life of comfort—and I mean spiritual comfort, not material comfort—there must be some force that helps us to do all of the things that we are destined to do. And in order for us to accomplish those things, it helps every day, even if just for a few minutes, to pray to that supreme power, however you see it. Ask him, her, whoever it is, for guidance. Reading some spiritual books is helpful. In fact, I think it is one of the most useful things young people can do, because it helps them to understand their own religion and those of others.

How important do you think it is for people to study different traditions?

Until we learn to respect other religions, we cannot claim that we ourselves are truly religious. Even though we say we are Christian or Hindu or Muslim, we believe that our God is the same one. At the same time, we have each chosen our own path to understanding that God. The mind is too small, and life is too short, for us ever to fully understand God. So some people decide not to try. They pray to no one. They give up. And then all they have is anger. In order for us to live the best life we can, I think we must follow a religion, whichever one gives us the maximum comfort in terms of connecting ourselves to the supreme power we relate to.

Do you think it's important for people to remain in the spiritual tradition they were raised in or born into? For example, do you think Westerners can get something out of becoming Hindu?

I'm sure that they can. Very sure. I have spoken to many Westerners who are following Hinduism. Many of them come to our temple. The one thing they have in common is that they could not find inner peace in the religion they were following, but they can find it in Hinduism. Like I said before, everyone should follow one religion. But it doesn't matter what it is, in my opinion. If that person was born or raised Christian but didn't feel connected to it, and instead found something in Buddhism or Hinduism or any other religion that helped him understand himself and his life more fully, then that is what is important. He will be a better person for that. The very fact that he is following *any* religion is wonderful.

As a medical doctor, where do you see the place for spirituality and religion in medicine?

I think spirituality should have a strong presence in all healing traditions. A good example of that is a practice that is becoming very popular here. It is called Vedic healing. Vedic healing is based on the recitation of Vedas—holy scriptures—that are supposed to encourage healing. It is believed that saying the Vedas creates enormous vibrations of energy, which are so powerful that they can bring about nuclear changes in the various molecules that make up the body.

Can you give an example of when your own work as a doctor has been helped by your spiritual practice?

In my own experience as a physician I have come across many serious situations, sometimes in the operating

Dr. Uma Mysorekar

room, where I feel the need to take a few minutes to stop and pray, chant, and speak to Lord Ganesha. And he has never let me down. That is one way.

You can tell a patient, "This is your sickness and here is the medication for it. Take it and go home and you will be fine." When you do that, it has some effect. But if you sit and talk to the patient, explaining to him what his sickness is all about, that helps even more. This is especially true of people who constantly worry about their health. These people are afraid that sickness means death. If you sit with them and explain to them the natural things that happen in life and that happen to our bodies, they begin to understand themselves. Then you teach them that prayer and chanting and meditation can help them understand even more.

Life is so short. We come today and we go tomorrow, and nobody knows when it will be over. And when we give patients a way to understand their life, it has a far greater effect on their healing than simply giving them a prescription and telling them to go home. Many of my patients come back to me later, not for medication, but to talk. They will say, "I'm having this problem, what might help it?" That is another way that my spirituality enters my profession.

Was this something that you were taught as part of your medical training, or did you develop it later?

I was taught it. Not so much in the curriculum in medical school, but at home. My mother used to say to me, "There are two aspects of medicine. One is the prescription, and the other is compassion." That compassion only comes if you have a mind based in spirituality, because otherwise you don't appreciate somebody else's suffering. Not necessarily their physical sickness, but any psychological suffering that might be adding to their trouble. Things that drugs and prescriptions alone cannot cure.

The day that I left to come to the United States, my mother said, "Do not ever forget the compassion and the sympathy and the understanding that you have learned." I have never forgotten that. If you listen to your patients, you have won half the battle.

Have there been aspects of the Hindu belief system that you have struggled with? For example, not being encouraged to become a doctor because you are a woman?

People have the incorrect notion that Hindu women face a lot of oppression. Now, unfortunately, there are some places where traditions such as the dowry system are still in place, where a woman is essentially treated as a piece of property to be exchanged in marriage. Although the government has tried to put a stop to it, there are still some villages where it is common. But that is a cultural thing, and not a part of Hindu tradition.

Have you ever had moments in your life when you thought that your beliefs simply weren't true, or that you had doubts?

Not doubts, exactly. But there are times when people treat you very badly, either in your profession or in your business, or even in your temple, a place of worship where you are volunteering your time. They sometimes make derogatory remarks or mistreat you. And then you wonder why. You think, "Here I am, leading to the best of my knowledge and ability a pure, conscious life, a cosmic life, a righteous life. I haven't hurt anybody. I haven't cheated anybody or stolen anything from anybody. And still I have to go through this. Why?"

And how do you deal with that?

There is a theory called the karmic theory. This is connected to the idea of reincarnation, and it is the belief that we all have to go through our particular karma in each lifetime. For example, if I am suffering in this life, it is because of past misdeeds I performed in my previous life. In this lifetime I must learn the lessons I did not learn the last time. And as I do so I accumulate righteousness in this life, so that in the next one I will not have to go through the same lessons.

Does believing that you are working toward something like that help you in your daily life?

If we sit here and say that all of the things that happen to us are negative, and therefore why does God exist if he is going to make us suffer, then we are defeating the purpose of spirituality. If we start with the belief that God created us and helps us along our way, then we must believe that he will give us the power and the strength to get through what we need to get through in this life.

I still go through rough periods like anyone else does. But over the years I have developed a way of looking at things. Sometimes my friends will say things like, "You spend so much time at the temple. You are so devoted to this. Why do people treat you badly? Don't you think that is unfair?" And no, it is not unfair. Because it could be a lot worse. So any time that I have moments when I wonder if God is with me, I remember that my life is much lighter than it could be. I remind myself that I am not doing these things to please other people. I am doing them for God.

Sometimes, though, it's hard to separate the followers from the religion and remember that those people treating you badly are not what the religion is really about.

Yes, and that's a very human problem. Jealousy is a human emotion. But sometimes when people see you doing what they wish they were doing or could do—especially when it comes to spiritual matters—they can try to bring you down.

Dr. Uma Mysorekar   179

Does it bother you that women cannot be Hindu priests?

One of the main reasons that only men used to be priests was that the job of the priest was a very difficult one because it was based largely on the chanting of the Vedas. The people who chant have to hold their breath for a very long time. It is much like yoga and can be very, very difficult. For a long time it was thought that women couldn't do that. Secondly, when a priest officiates, it involves lifting heavy vessels. It is very physical work. So taking these things into consideration, it is understandable that many thousands of years ago it was believed that only men should do these things. But that is changing now. Women still do not teach in temples. However, there are certain rituals done at home, for instance, that women lead.

Does it bother you, though, that you can reach a position like being the president of the Temple Society but you couldn't be a priest if you wanted to?

I really believe that God has given certain jobs to certain people. Men are good at certain things. Women are good at certain things. Why do we have to compete? I think this creates unnecessary tension and is a waste of time. If something is one person's job, then let her do it. If it's someone else's job, let him do it. Worrying about who does what doesn't do anyone any good. One must never believe that women are degraded or demeaned because they are not given the priesthood. That is the wrong way of thinking, because there are many things that are just as important as serving as priests that women do that men do not.

What does being a Hindu mean to you?

There is no one way to say what a Hindu is. We do not have a definition. There is no one scripture that we consider the only scripture, like a Bible or a Koran. Each of our holy books gives us a part of who we are. Essentially, to me, a Hindu is someone who is a good human being. Someone who is good to himself and good to his fellow beings. That is the most important aspect, because when you serve your community, you serve God.

What, then, is the point of living a life as a Hindu?

The goal for every Hindu is what we call salvation. To us, this means going to be with God. It is believed that anyone who has followed the most righteous way of life will not be reborn again, because she or he will go to be with God, probably by becoming a star in the sky. However, there are people who live good, righteous lives who *are* reborn, for the simple reason that you need good people in the world to straighten out the bad people. If everybody is bad and struggling, then the whole world will be bad. So we believe that good souls are sometimes reborn to teach us. They are the sages and wise people who return in various places to help us learn how to apply the teachings of Hinduism to our life.

We believe that when we die, it is only the physical body that dies. The astral body, the soul, migrates and merges with God to await rebirth. Sometimes, we believe, that soul is reborn into the same family it lived with before, and sometimes it is reborn into a different family. Depending upon the person's deeds in the old life, she or he will be in a better life or a harder life. If the soul is reborn into a good life, it is a celebration of the good deeds done in the last one. If the soul is born into a difficult life, it is thought to be the result of misdeeds done in the last life.

Do you see reincarnation as a system of punishment and reward, then?

There is one thing that I believe, and that is that God does not punish anyone. We must each pay our own debts and accept the consequences of what we do in our life. God cannot absorb everybody's sins. But he can teach us lessons that will help us learn what we need to, so that we can help ourselves.

Do you ever let yourself think about what your next life might be like?

No, I don't. Because I feel that if I can accomplish the best that I can in this life, then the next life will be what

Paths of Faith

is meant to be. I can only do the best I can, and then I trust God to decide what I should be or shouldn't be in the next.

Now, does being the best person you can be mean being someone who has accomplished great things?

There is a very important man in Hinduism, Swami Vivekananda. He was the first person ever to address a large gathering in America, where he was the representative of Hinduism at the World Parliament of Religions held in Chicago in 1893. He was a very poor man. But he firmly believed in his goal, and he had tremendous knowledge and determination. He was a follower of Ramakrishna, the greatest Hindu saint.

When he was growing up, his horoscope—which is very important in Hindu culture—was not very auspicious. But when he grew, under the influence of this great saint and the teachings, his whole life changed. He is now considered the greatest teacher in the Hindu tradition. So the predictions for our lives are not necessarily set in stone. They can change if we believe they can change, through spirituality and faith. And your success can be no less whether you are a beggar or a king. As long as you are a true human being, you have succeeded.

What has been, for you, the most rewarding part of a life spent in the Hindu faith?

Dr. Uma Mysorekar   183

Inner peace. The peace and the tranquility. Most of all, my faith gives me tremendous strength in my day-to-day work.

What has been the most challenging part of a life spent in the Hindu faith?

Trying to convey the teachings to other people who might not understand them. For example, trying to help young people understand why it is important to follow and to faithfully practice our teachings. It is hard to understand sometimes, when you are young, why something that may seem so difficult is so useful to you. But I know, from my own life, how fulfilling and how necessary it is, and I want to be able to show that to others.

FOR MORE INFORMATION

ON-LINE RESOURCES

Hindu Resources Online
www.hindu.org

The Hindu Universe
www.hindunet.org

Both of these sites are excellent places to begin looking for information about Hinduism on-line. They feature

Paths of Faith

links to Hindu organizations, lists of Hindu temples across the country, and information about Hindu deities and beliefs.

BOOKS

The Bhagavad Gita, translated by Eknath Easwaran (Nilgiri Press, 1985). Of all the Hindu scriptures, this is unquestionably the most central. There are many different translations of it. This particular one contains introductions to each chapter that explain the concepts in a way that is easy to follow for those trying to get a better understanding of this classic religious text.

Hidden Journey, by Andrew Harvey (Penguin, 1992). Probably the most accessible and certainly one of the most poetic accounts of a Westerner's spiritual journey into Indian mysticism.

My Guru and His Disciple, by Christopher Isherwood (Noonday Press, 1996). Isherwood, a well-known English writer, met Swami Prabhavananda while living and working in Hollywood during World War II. This autobiography describes how exploring the beliefs of Hinduism made an impact on his view of the world.

Hinduism (Teach Yourself World Faiths series), by V. P. Kanitkar and W. Owen Cole (Hodder & Stoughton,

1995). This practical book offers a guide to Hindu beliefs, forms of worship, and the values and customs of the Hindu community.

Loving Ganesha, by Satguru Sivaya Subramuniyaswami (Himalayan Academy Publications, n.d.). An all-you-wanted-to-know-but-were-afraid-to-ask book about Ganesha, the divine and much-loved remover of obstacles in the Hindu religion. Ganesha is the deity Dr. Mysorekar discusses in her interview.

Am I a Hindu? by Ed Viswanathan (Halo Books, 1992). This book uses a conversational format to cover a range of Hindu beliefs, answering questions Westerners ask about Hindu practice, including What exactly is the law of karma and reincarnation? Why do Hindu women wear a red dot on their forehead? and Why do Hindus worship so many gods?

Autobiography of a Yogi, by Paramahansa Yogananda (Self-realization Fellowship, 1979). Considered a classic in its field since it was first published in 1946, Yogananda's autobiography reveals the sentiments and teachings of one of the teachers who helped spread Eastern knowledge in the West.

Stephen Cary

Member, the Religious Society of Friends

*"I am profoundly committed to my Quaker faith. . . .
I never feel that I'm part of a remnant of a religion. I
feel much more that I'm part of a pioneering group
that believes that we can move in a different direction."*

The Religious Society of Friends, more commonly called
simply the Friends or the Quakers, was founded in the
seventeenth century in England by George Fox
(1624–1691). Fox was a spiritual seeker who did not find
answers to his questions in any of the churches of his day.
In particular he believed that the spirit of God was present in every human being, and that people did not need
priests and bishops, or any other religious leaders, to tell
them the truth of God or to do the work of God. He
spoke out against the church as a hierarchical institution
and against the oppression of people on account of race,
sex, or class. These views were, to say the least, not very

popular with the Catholic or Anglican Churches, which largely controlled religious life of that time, and Fox found himself persecuted for speaking about his beliefs.

Originally, Fox did not set out to start his own faith. He attempted to get the existing churches to return to what he saw as the true plan for the Christian faith as expressed by Jesus Christ. But when the existing churches failed to embrace his message, and after having a visionary experience, he founded the Religious Society of Friends. The name *Friends* came from the scripture "You are my friends / if you do what I command you" (John 15:14). The label *Quaker* was first used as a derogatory nickname because early Friends urged those who heard their message to tremble in the face of the power of the Lord.

The society rapidly grew in popularity and, through the work of Quaker missionaries, spread to many different countries, including the United States, where Quaker missionaries first landed in Boston in 1656. But the Quakers were not received well in America, and many were imprisoned, attacked, and fined for preaching their beliefs. Some of them, including Mary Dyer, the first woman to die for her faith on these shores, were hanged in Boston Common between 1659 and 1661. Despite this opposition, and because of increasing religious persecution in England, Quakers continued to come to America and slowly made inroads. By the time the Civil War ended, Quaker settlements could be found from coast to coast.

The essential teachings of the Quakers are founded on the idea that religion is an experiential journey, meaning that each person has to find the answers to her or his questions by being continually aware of life's processes and God's role in them. While Quakerism is definitely a Christian faith, there is no creed and no set church doctrine about the role of Christ in believers' lives.

The fundamental Quaker belief is that each person has inherited some of God's power, or light, and that by using these powers accordingly to do God's work, that light is strengthened and grows. They believe that the Bible should not be taken as the final revelation of God, but that each person should hear the message of God and listen to how it speaks to him or her personally. Quaker worship services are called meetings, and their churches are called meetinghouses. Quakers have no church hierarchy or clergy in the traditional sense, although they do recognize that some Friends, both male and female, are gifted with the skills of pastoring, and those people may be asked to lead meetings and teach others.

The Quakers have, from the outset, been committed to social causes. They have always seen women and men as being equal, and have worked against oppression of all kinds. They are perhaps best known for their commitment to peace and nonviolence. This commitment to pacifism has often put Quakers in conflict with the governments of the countries in which they live, and particularly became an issue of public policy and debate

Stephen Cary

in America during World Wars I and II, when many Quaker men refused to participate in armed service.

As a result, the Friends were instrumental in creating alternative ways for those committed to pacifism to serve their country. The most well-known Quaker peace organization to come out of that time is the American Friends Service Committee (AFSC), which was founded in 1917 to provide conscientious objectors with an opportunity to aid civilian victims during World War I, and which is still in operation today, working for peace around the world. Stephen Cary is a Friend who was very active in one of the most successful programs to be developed during World War II, the Civilian Public Service, and who later worked for the AFSC.

How did you come to be involved with the Friends?

I didn't have much choice—I was born into the Friends. My mother and father were both Quakers. But I wasn't particularly drawn to it when I was young. Even though I went to Quaker meetings from the time that I was four or five, I wasn't seriously involved during my years in school or even in college. I was much more interested in sports and extracurricular activities. It really wasn't until I was faced with the possibility of military draft that I had to make a decision about my beliefs. When the clouds of World War II began to gather, I realized along with several million other young men of my age that we would soon be called to fight on the battlefield. It was at that time that I began to think seriously about what I should do.

How did you come to a decision?

Several things influenced me. One was a call from my family in the fall of 1940. My father worked for a company that manufactured high-efficiency temperature controls for machinery. He had always said that he would continue to stay with the company as long as they didn't get into the business of manufacturing weaponry. Then his company accepted a contract to build a component used in bombing technology. My father didn't believe that, as a Quaker committed to nonviolence, he could continue to work there. But he didn't want to quit without our permission, because it was going to completely change our lifestyle.

Of course we told him that he should do what he thought was right, and the next day he quit. The thing that rocked me about it was that the company was his life. He was an executive vice president. He had worked there for thirty-five years, helping to build it from a very tiny company into a very successful one. He poured his whole life into it. Yet when it came into conflict with his convictions, he didn't hesitate a minute. He quit. This really shook me up. I thought, "Here is a man who really is committed to Quaker beliefs. Where do I stand on

Stephen Cary

these things?" That's the first time I really began to think about it.

Why are the Friends so committed to nonviolence?

We believe that each human being has the capacity to know the will of God directly. For Friends this is one of the pillars of our peace testimony. The capacity to communicate directly with God, we believe, gives a sacred dimension to life. Therefore, life cannot be debased, exploited, or destroyed for any reason. The Friends feel that the teachings of Jesus in this area are unequivocal and cannot be compromised. We believe that Jesus was very clear when he said that love overcomes, and that love is the only way to overcome evil. The Friends have believed in this from the very beginning. They wrote to King Charles II in 1660 saying that they were not going to fight with weapons under any conditions for the kingdom of this world.

So being directly confronted with that same scenario at the outset of World War II put you in a similar situation?

Yes. Another thing that influenced me were the teachings that I'd had as a young man. Although I didn't think I was paying a lot of attention then, all of a sudden they started to surface. I began to ask myself a lot of questions. I had to decide whether or not I called myself a Christian. And if I did, what did that mean? I was struggling with that. I had my father's example to follow as well. All of these things were getting me to start examining what I believed.

At the time, I was living at a YMCA. One night I was having a cup of coffee down in the lounge, and I overheard the conversation of a group of four men at the next table. They were talking about Quakers, the war, and the American Friends Service Committee. I decided to go join the conversation. As it turned out, three of the guys had recently accepted commissions in what at that time was called the Army Air Force. They were waiting to be called to duty. The other man was a brilliant young Quaker philosopher. They were having a conversation about the conflict between citizenship and faith, and where the balance was. It was a marvelous discussion, and it went on over three nights. Mostly I just listened to these men talk. But it had quite an influence on me. By the time the fourth night came, it became very clear to me that because of my father's example, because of the lessons and teachings I'd learned as a Quaker, and because of what we'd talked about in that conversation, I simply could not kill.

Were you eventually drafted?

Very shortly after I made my decision, I was drafted. It was the fall of 1941. It was before Pearl Harbor, but *just* before.

Stephen Cary   193

Did you have any difficulties with your draft board when you told them you wouldn't fight?

I had relatively little trouble, probably because I was in Philadelphia, where there are a lot of Quakers. They knew our beliefs. When I was drafted, they tried to persuade me to go into the military in some noncombatant capacity. But I felt I couldn't do that because if I took any noncombat job in the military, it would mean someone else would have to take my job as a soldier.

Were you afraid of what might happen to you for refusing to sign up?

I was afraid of going to prison, which is where they could have sent me. But I am grateful that the government had, for the first time in its history, provided an alternative for conscientious objectors. I decided that I would accept that alternative service, the Civilian Public Service, which was a rather unlikely marriage between what were called the peace churches—Friends, Brethren, and Mennonites—and the selective service system. It was an alternative to war duty.

Did a lot of men choose the Civilian Public Service?

I think there were between 12,000 and 14,000 young men in the Civilian Public Service. Not all of them came from the peace churches. Many were simply men who were pacifists for one reason or another. There were another 7,000 who chose instead to go to prison and not support the war effort in any way. We had Pulitzer Prize winners working alongside men with third-grade educations. We had Fundamentalists, Evangelicals, atheists, ballet dancers, lawyers. We had farm boys who worked like dogs and guys who could barely lift a brick. It was incredibly diverse. The men who decided to join the Civilian Public Service lived in work camps together. The camps were way out in the sticks where the general public couldn't see them. In fact, they were old Civilian Conservation Corps camps left over from the days of Franklin Delano Roosevelt.

Why did they hide the camps?

They didn't want this to be a popular option for conscientious objectors. They deliberately made it so that it wouldn't be attractive. The work was sometimes difficult and always very dull. The biggest thing was we weren't paid. We received $2.50 a month each from the churches, but nothing from the government.

Between the difficult work and no pay, how did people handle it?

For people who, like myself, came from a reasonably well-to-do background and had resources, the no-pay feature wasn't such an issue. But for the guy who came from an unsympathetic household and was poor to

Stephen Cary   195

begin with, it was very hard. He had to work for nothing for four years.

Were you always kept away from the general public?

At first, yes. The camps were far back in the woods. They did develop what they called detached service. The men were all sent first to the camps to begin with. But after strenuous negotiations with the selective service we were eventually able to get the men involved in other projects. Some were involved in various medical experiments. Some were trained as smoke jumpers, who parachuted into forest fires. That was extremely popular. I think we had about six hundred guys apply for thirty positions. But the greatest contributions made during that time were in the area of mental hospitals.

How so?

Well, working in mental hospitals was such unpleasant work that the selective service was willing to approve it as something that conscientious objectors could do. Mental hospitals at the time were seriously understaffed. The care of the mentally ill was absolutely terrible. Then suddenly there was an infusion of hundreds and hundreds of these idealistic young men, who completely revolutionized the care of the mentally ill in the United States and made permanent changes. They founded mental health organizations that still exist today, and the standard of care in public hospitals increased dramatically. It was probably our single greatest contribution.

What was your own personal work in the Civilian Public Service?

I was very fortunate. I became a camp director. I directed three camps, which was an enormously difficult job. It took all of my abilities to manage such a diverse group of people. Half the guys were trying to work like dogs to show the government that they were sincere in wanting to help, and half regarded themselves as slave labor and wanted to show the government that it couldn't force slaves to work. So half were working hard and half were doing as little as they could. And I was in the middle of this as the director. But despite it all, I had a wonderful experience. I learned a lot about how to deal with people and how to administer in impossible situations.

World War II was an incredibly popular war. What was the public's reaction to your work, which was essentially antiwar work?

Actually, we had reasonably good relations with civilians. Sometimes the wives of conscientious objectors would be fired from their jobs when it was learned that their husbands were COs. But it wasn't terribly bad. As far as the military was concerned, we got along with them. The only people who really caused us problems were the veterans of World War I. They sometimes appointed themselves as vigilantes and caused trouble. But our relations with the communities weren't too bad. Obviously it was something I did worry about.

How did all of this affect your spiritual life?

When you have 150 guys in a camp stuck off in the woods, with no money and nowhere to go for four years, you learn a lot. We argued, debated, and discussed what we would do in situations ranging from what to do when someone is being raped, to how to deal with the situations in the world. We discussed everything you can think of. As a result, it was the best training ground for maturing and for forcing people to think about their spiritual positions that ever was devised. I emerged a much more convinced Friend and much more committed pacifist, as did many others. Graduates of Civilian Public Service staffed the peace movement for the next fifty years.

When it became very clear what Hitler was doing during World War II—killing millions of people—did you have moments when you wondered how God could let it happen?

Some men did. Some guys left Civilian Public Service and went into the military when they saw what was happening. Some felt the churches were making too big of a compromise with the military and walked out of the camps to go to jail instead. As far as I was concerned, I didn't have any doubts. First of all, there comes a time when you do something because you don't have any other answers and you simply have to trust God that you're doing the right thing.

The other thing that I kept in mind was that for years, and for centuries, Quakers have been working on the problems of peace and justice. When the First World War ended, the Quakers knocked themselves out trying to push for a fair peace agreement. The Quakers fed a million children in Germany in 1920 and 1921 because nobody else would do it. It was our argument that had a decent peace plan been developed at the end of World War I, the bitter soil out of which Hitler rose would never have been developed.

The Friends felt that for us to be required to have answers for what was happening in 1939 was unrealistic. If things after World War I had been done the way we suggested, and if Hitler had still risen to power, and if we had then gone to General Eisenhower and said, "Save us from Hitler," he would have told us we were too late. People would have said, "Look, we tried it your way for thirty years and it didn't work. Don't expect us to solve your problem."

But that was exactly what the government was asking us to do by fighting in World War II. They were asking

Stephen Cary   199

us to solve the problem they'd created by the way they had handled the peace settlement after World War I. In 1939 the Friends said, "Look, we have been advocating a wholly different approach to the problem of Germany. You have totally ignored us. Now you come to us and ask us to help you. Well, it's too late."

That's a negative argument, but it made sense. But I would hasten to tell you that the fundamental belief that influenced my decision was that, as a Christian, I had to make a choice between whether I was going to try to follow the example of Jesus or if I wasn't. If I wasn't, then I knew I had to give all of it up, and I didn't want that. I wanted to be a follower of Christ. It was a conviction rooted in religion, and I just had to follow it.

Many people might assume that you made a choice not to fight out of a fear of dying. Was that part of it?

No, it really wasn't. And when it was all over, I clearly felt that I had a responsibility to the veterans who did fight. My friends had been shot at, had killed and been killed, and I had escaped all that. As a result, I volunteered for two more years in relief service. So the war cost me six years, not four.

What really changed my whole life was that I was offered a job overseeing Quaker relief for the American Friends Service Committee in Europe in the years right after the Second World War. For two years I wandered over the face of Europe, and there are very few people who saw the price we paid for war the way I saw it. I encountered great suffering. The whole social fabric of countries was wiped out, and there was unbelievable destruction of the continent. But most of all there was the cold, the hungry, the homeless, and the bereaved.

It was a searing experience, and more than ever confirmed for me that I had made the right choice. More than that, it convinced me that I could never go back and work in the business world. I had been planning on a business career. But after those two years in Europe I had no desire to go back to that. I knew I had to spend the rest of my life working on issues of peace and justice, to try to prevent such a thing from ever happening again.

Did you ever have moments of doubt about the workings of God when you saw these things?

No, I didn't, because what God gave us was freedom of choice. That's a great gift. I didn't blame God for what had happened, I blamed people who used their freedom of choice in wrong ways. I felt that the war was a result of human failure, not God's failure. Maybe the reason that I didn't have those doubts, while others did, was because Friends don't believe that God spoke only once and that everything he said is in the Scriptures. We believe that he continues to speak to us today. We believe that we are very imperfect vessels who receive his word and his will very imperfectly, but we do believe that we continue to receive new fragments of truth when we listen. Quakerism is a searching religion, searching for new insights and new truths. It is not a religion where you have one particular creed that once you accept it, you're in good shape and are going to go to heaven.

Is it like the Jewish faith, where there is a tradition of arguing with God?

Not exactly. We question more our interpretations of God than what God says. My whole life has been based on the possibility that the human being is redeemable. There is always the possibility of redemption, and I believe that people *can* live in a better way. I have been very optimistic, even in the face of evidence to the contrary. I am profoundly committed to my Quaker faith, and I believe that I can grow and learn more truths, that I can be more successful in fighting for what I believe in and working for what I believe in. I never feel that I'm part of a remnant of a religion. I feel much more that I'm part of a pioneering group that believes that we can move in a different direction.

That's an interesting point, because I think many people have the idea that Quakerism is a very stuffy tradition. They picture the man on the box of Quaker Oats and think that Quakers are all grim people who sit around in old churches being silent.

When in fact it's very vibrant. In a sense, for three hundred years we have not tried to debate our pacifism, we have lived it. We have been out there trying to find creative ways to deal with problems in the world, where hatred has made things worse. We have worked with the marginalized, the refugees, victims of discrimination, migrant workers. All of these people. And we have worked in some of the toughest war situations around. So I think our money is where our mouth is.

Have you ever imagined a situation in which you would physically fight for something?

What I have always said is that were I to be tested, I cannot know for certain how I would react. All I know is that if I did turn to killing, it would be my failure. It would be my lack of courage and my failure in trying to find new insight and creative ways to handle the situation. I might fight. I believe in a police force. I do believe that when people get off the track, you need to have order and law in society. I think there's a huge difference between a police force and an army. The police force is an arresting force, not the judge, jury, and executioner. I have often wondered what I would do if, for example, my wife were being attacked. Yes, I would intervene. I would use force to stop it. I would not kill. I would hope that I am ready to be killed rather than kill. But I can't promise that.

Do you think that people misunderstand pacifism and assume that it's just an excuse for cowardice?

I think they sometimes feel it's simply standing aside and letting other people do the dirty work. But to be worth anything, pacifism has to be active. It has to be proactive, and it has to have a proven track record of working to prevent violence and advance peace. And pacifism does have that record, so it's against that background that I think pacifists have the right to say no to violence. Because nonviolence works. I couldn't claim in 1940 much of a track record in peace work myself. But I was the inheritor of my ancestors' efforts in peace work.

After working with the AFSC you went to teach at Haverford College. Why did you go from active peace work to a more academic environment?

That was an interesting transition. I worked for the AFSC for twenty-two years after World War II. I had two small children, and it was a terrible strain on my wife. For example, in 1965 I was sent out to Vietnam at the height of the war to develop a Friends relief program in South Vietnam. I saw the war firsthand and was working in the middle of war situations. That was hard on my family, and I thought it wasn't fair to put that burden on them.

In the course of living amid suffering and violence, and the wake of violence, one can't help but get ideas and insights into what it is that makes for peace and what makes for war, what creates justice and what creates injustice. You start to understand what qualities a person needs to be a reconciler in the midst of such situations. Many times I saw our workers fail, and I saw myself fail. We could feed a community and clothe a community. We could build a water system and houses. But we couldn't reach through the hatred and the bitterness and the anger that sear the soul and block any hope for reconciliation and healing. But I also saw miracles happen, and I started to ask myself what was making the difference. It was the qualities of life that people brought to their jobs.

In analyzing that, I identified three or four of these qualities and decided that people who had them were in mighty short supply. I thought that maybe, having worked in the field seeing people struggling to work for peace, I could contribute to teaching these qualities to others. That's why I went to Haverford College, which is a Quaker college. I saw it as an opportunity to turn out young graduates who, in addition to competence, had certain other qualities of life that would help them contribute to the cause of peace. So I did

Stephen Cary

administrative work and taught classes in international mediation, dealing with mediating not only conflicts between countries but also conflicts with radical groups based in fanaticism and irrational thought.

So after all this time do you still believe the things that first stirred you to live out your Quaker beliefs?

If anything, I believe in them more strongly now. I'm not nearly as involved as I once was. I mean, I haven't been to jail for some time now. But I have gone to jail for my beliefs on several occasions.

What for?

For peaceful protests. I went to jail first, I think, in Washington over the issue of free food stamps. I'd been in Memphis, Tennessee, and seen American children with their stomachs distended because of lack of food. Their families didn't qualify for food stamps under the government guidelines, and they were starving to death in a country with more food than we knew what to do with. We were pouring fifty billion dollars into Vietnam, and children were starving. I thought this was absolutely unconscionable. So I marched in Washington, and we ended up getting arrested for refusing to leave the grounds of the Capitol. I think I got three weeks in jail. It caused quite a bit of publicity,

Paths of Faith

and the next day a whole new group of people came down to protest and were arrested. And over the next few months it raised a lot of attention, and eventually legislation was passed to give these people food stamps.

The only time I ever tried to obstruct anything was late in the Vietnam War, when I felt that people were doing what they were told instead of what they believed in. During that time I lay down on a railroad track to prevent bombs from being delivered to a navy yard. That was a very important experience for me.

Do you think participating in social action is an important part of spirituality?

I think that human freedom—the things that we enjoy and so often take for granted, like freedom of speech, freedom of assembly, freedom of worship, the right to a jury trial—all of these fundamental foundations of freedom have, for the most part, not been won on the battlefield. They have been won by people saying no. What's the point of someone being burned at the stake for standing up for his religious beliefs? What was the point of Jesus going to the cross? If you make a witness for and are faithful to your beliefs, it makes people think. The aim is not to beat someone in a battle; it's to make them think. When I lay down on that railroad track, my goal was to say, "Why are we sending 500-pound bombs to the battleship *New Jersey* off the coast of Vietnam to be lobbed, from a position of total security, into a rice paddy thirty miles away?" In my view, it is the witness of one or two people that begins a process of change. If you trace the things that I've talked about, the freedoms we enjoy, you will find that people died for them, and usually at times when society thought that fighting for those rights was silly.

It may seem awfully silly to make a witness, especially if only one or a few of you are doing it. But how else do things change? From my standpoint, it may seem foolish to stand up for what you think is right, but it's the only way change is going to come. And if I don't do it, who else is going to do it? One person can stand up and make an impact. Look at Rosa Parks. One woman refused to take a seat in the back of the bus. And that one woman ignited a whole city, and then a whole country.

What have you gotten out of a lifetime of being involved in the Quaker faith?

A wonderful, happy life. I never feel that I'm struggling or in agony. I've had an exhilarating time. I've enjoyed life, I've made some small contributions to it, and I find personal satisfaction in trying to live with integrity. I've had many backslides, but the effort to try is enormously satisfying. It's satisfying to say, "Yes, I tried to help in Europe." I've worked with the AFSC alongside farm workers, and with Native Americans and inner-city kids. Those things are fun.

Do you ever think about what will be waiting for you when you die?

I'm prepared to leave that to God. I don't think I can even begin to fathom that one. All I can do is try to live a useful life. I don't think about it much because I think that if I do the best I can here on Earth, the future will take care of itself. I don't know about a hell or a heaven. I think whatever happens to me, I'll be satisfied with that, and maybe I'll get a chance to meet some of the people I've loved dearly in this life. I think it's a waste of time to believe that if you follow certain statements or practices that it will ensure salvation. You can waste your whole life trying to live up to that.

How do you see your relationship to God at this point in your life?

My motivation is really rooted in trying to be a devoted follower of Jesus. It's terribly important to me that he was *not* the Son of God. If he was the Son of God, then he's running on a different track than the one I'm on. He has no right to come up and tell me that I have to follow him. I think he earned the right, by the quality of his life and what he did, to be seen as the nearest thing we have to someone who is in the image of God. I would say that my roots are very, very deep in faith and in the message of Jesus. And I think they have to be. If you're going to have the courage to stand, it isn't enough just to be ethical. I think you have to have faith. Again, I don't have any assurance that I would be able to stand up if push came to shove. All I know is that I'm trying.

What is your advice to young people exploring their own spirituality?

Get involved in something. Go down and feed people at a soup kitchen. Volunteer for some kind of service project in your community. From my standpoint, there's nothing that builds one's faith so much as getting involved in something that helps other people. Don't keep it in your head. Go out and do something. Because no matter which way it goes, the experience will enrich you.

FOR MORE INFORMATION

ON-LINE RESOURCES

American Friends Service Committee
www.afsc.org

Founded in 1917 to provide conscientious objectors with an opportunity to aid civilian victims during World War I, today the AFSC runs programs that focus on issues related to economic justice, peace building and demilitarization, social justice, and youth. Its Web site contains numerous links and is also the site for the Quaker Information Center.

The Religious Society of Friends
www.quaker.org

This is the most comprehensive collection of information about Quakerism, and contains links to many different sites, including publishers, periodicals, and Quaker youth organizations.

Peaceweb
www.web.net/~peaceweb

Peaceweb is a Quaker Web page on peace and the social concerns of Friends. It features information about Quaker positions on, and responses to, issues of education, violence, child welfare, and economic concerns.

BOOKS

The best books on Quakers and the Quaker experience are published by Quaker presses, particularly Pendle Hill Publications. Although many of the books listed below were first published a number of years ago, they continue to be the best sources of information about Quakerism. Pendle Hill also publishes an ongoing series of booklets related to Quaker life, beliefs, and positions on social issues. You can find a link to Pendle Hill Publications on the Religious Society of Friends Web site. Their books are also found in libraries and may be ordered through bookstores.

The Quiet Rebels: The Story of the Quakers in America, by Margaret H. Bacon (New Society, 1985). The history of the Friends upon their arrival in America.

Friends for 300 Years, by Howard H. Brinton (Pendle Hill, 1965). An outline of the history and beliefs of the Religious Society of Friends since George Fox started the movement.

The Best of Friends, vol. 1, edited by Chuck Fager (Kimo Press, 1998). A wonderful collection of Quaker story-telling, some fiction and some nonfiction.

Hidden in Plain Sight: Quaker Women's Writings, 1650–1700, edited by Mary Garman, Judith Applegate, Margaret Benefiel, and Dortha Meredith (Pendle Hill, 1995). An anthology of memoirs, diaries, travelogues, and tracts that show the experience of women within the early Quaker movement.

Faith and Practice of the Quakers, by Rufus M. Jones (Friends United Press, 1980). A basic outline of the Quaker faith.

The Journals of George Fox, by John L. Nickalls (Philadelphia Yearly Meeting, 1995). The journals of the founder of the Religious Society of Friends.

The Quaker Reader, by Jessamyn West (Pendle Hill, 1992). This classic in Quaker reading contains excerpts from the writings of noted Quakers from 165 to 1992, including George Fox, William Penn, Elizabeth Fry, Margaret Fell, and others.

Gwendolyn Zoharah Simmons

Assistant Professor of Religion, University of Florida

"I love the notion that I am a divine spark from the creator, that I am a ray from the soul of God that has taken on a physical form for a period of time to learn certain things. Prayer time for me is very beautiful and very holy, and that is the thing I love most about Islam."

Islam was founded in A.D. 622 by Muhammad (or Mohammed), the Prophet (circa 570–632), after, it is believed, he was visited by the archangel Gabriel and became convinced that it was his duty to spread the message of God to his people. While some consider Islam to be the youngest of the world's old religions (which include Judaism, Christianity, and Hinduism), many followers of Islam feel that it is in reality the true version of the faith taught by the ancient prophets Abraham, David, Moses, and Jesus. They believe

214

Muhammad's role as the last of the prophets was to formalize and clarify the faith and to purify it by removing foreign ideas that had been added in error.

Followers of Islam are called Muslims, which is an Arabic word meaning "a person who submits to the will of God." Muslims refer to God as Allah, an Arabic word that means "the one true God." At an estimated population of 1.2 billion, Muslims represent about 22 percent of the world's people, making them the second largest religion in the world behind Christianity.

The two sacred texts of Islam are the Koran (or Qur'an) and the Hadith. The Koran is believed to be the direct word of God, revealed to the prophet Muhammad, while the Hadith is a collection of the sayings of Muhammad. Although there is no one set of beliefs that define all Muslim people, a Muslim's basic spiritual duties are called the "five pillars of Islam." They include believing in the *shahadah*, or creed, which is "There is no God but Allah and Muhammad is his Prophet"; performing prayer five times each day (which involves bowing and making prostrations while facing in the direction of the holy city of Mecca); donating regularly to the needy; fasting during the holy month of Ramadan; and, if at all possible, making the pilgrimage to Mecca during one's lifetime.

Islam has been greatly misunderstood by many people for a number of reasons. Because of divisions between different Islamic groups, the confusion of societal customs in some Islamic societies with actual Islamic religious beliefs, and political unrest in countries with largely Islamic populations, the religion has received an undeserved reputation for being overly violent and oppressive. But the majority of Muslims are peaceful, loving people who follow a spiritual path rich in history and tradition.

Gwendolyn Zoharah Simmons converted to Islam after becoming interested in Sufism, a branch of Islam devoted to mysticism and exploring questions about the nature of God. From the time she was a teenager and volunteered in the early civil rights movement, she has been involved in many different movements and organizations relating to human rights. Her interest in exploring Islam further led her to pursue her doctorate in religious studies, and she is now an assistant professor of religion at the University of Florida at Gainesville, specializing in Islam, African American religion, and women in religion.

What was your relationship to religion and spirituality as a young person?

I was born into Christianity and raised in a very devoutly Christian home. However, I was interested in mysticism from a very early age. Even as I was actively participating in my church, I had lots of questions that I felt were not being answered by the Christian teachings as taught to me.

Paths of Faith

What kinds of questions?

I can remember being about thirteen years old and asking people, "Who am I?" And they looked at me like I was crazy and answered, "What do you mean, who are you?" I learned after a while that you don't go around asking people those kinds of questions, because they don't understand. When I asked my grandmother, who was very religious, she said, "Stop asking crazy questions." I didn't really know myself what I meant by the question. I just knew it was there inside, that I had deep questions about what this life is really all about. I wanted to know why we are all here and who we all really are. I felt that just to be born, grow up, have a family, and die wasn't enough. I didn't understand why it had to happen like that and why we were in the world if that's all there was.

Why do you think you weren't getting answers to those questions in the church you attended?

As I've looked at religion as an adult I've realized that unless you are really interested in asking philosophical questions, it's easy not to ask them. Many people attend church or go to the synagogue or mosque and take the teachings they receive at face value, without ever questioning what's beneath them. In the church I attended as a young person, religion had much more to do with belief and faith than with grappling with the deep questions that human beings have had since the beginning of time.

Were you aware that there were Christian mystics who thought and wrote about these things?

Not at that time. I was not aware of them until I started really studying these issues. And of course what I then learned was that when you start getting to the mystical level of spirituality, there is an incredible unity among the religious traditions. But as a young person I wasn't encouraged to do that kind of thinking. I don't think most young people are. Many times when you ask these kinds of questions, you're told to go take a philosophy course or something, as if it's all theoretical. But for me, as a child, these were very real, burning questions, and they never went away. I was a very active person in school and in the rest of my life, so to some extent my search to answer these questions was sidelined by everyday life. But the questions were always there.

How did you come to be interested in Islam?

I grew up in Memphis, Tennessee, during the 1950s and 1960s, and became involved very early on in the civil rights movement. The sit-in movement and the Freedom Riders and all of those things were taking place

Paths of Faith

in my teenage years. But even though I was active in the civil rights movement—by participating in sit-ins and going to jail and all of that—whenever I had a little time to myself, I would look for books on mysticism, trying to answer the questions of my heart. Eventually this led me to try yoga, and that in turn led me to the teacher who introduced me to Sufism, Muhammad Raheen Bawa Muhaiyadeen. He was a Sufi sheikh, meaning a divinely wise teacher, who had come from Sri Lanka to the United States. I happened to be part of a yoga group that learned of his coming and was at the Philadelphia airport to meet him in 1971. From the moment I saw him I felt a very deep connection. He began to answer the questions that I had had for so long, questions like: Who am I, meaning at the most profound level? Who is God? And what is the relationship between the two? Through him I began a study of the mystical stream of Islam—Sufism.

Do you think growing up in the midst of the civil rights movement had any effect on your search to answer these questions?

I remember talking once to Bob Moses, who was very famous during the civil rights era for his involvement in the Student Nonviolent Coordinating Committee. He is a very spiritual person, and he was the leader of the Mississippi project of SNCC, which is a project I volunteered for during the summer of 1964. It

Gwendolyn Zoharah Simmons

was the summer that the three civil rights workers were murdered: Schwerner, Goodman, and Chaney. I was talking to Bob about spirituality, and I said, "What does this all mean? We're activists, and we've been on the front lines, yet we've also always had this yearning on a spiritual level." Bob, who is also interested in yoga, said, "All I know is that this is one yogi who also went to Mississippi." I think the yearning for justice, for basic decency and treating people with kindness, was always deep in my heart. I'm sure these two things must be connected, but I'm not sure I can say how exactly.

Did the horrors that occurred during the civil rights movement ever make you doubt that there was a God or a higher power?

I certainly can remember wondering how or why God would let certain things happen. And of course in my case there was this desire to get to the root of all these questions, to find out what was behind it all. I would say now that I saw the world as a great stage and we were all actors on it, but I wanted to know who was putting on the play and directing it, and why. I wanted to know why there was poverty and suffering for so many, and tremendous wealth for so few. These are the questions that continue to drive me, and lead me to keep studying. Within the mystical stream of Islam I have begun to discover answers to those questions. I know I have not found them all yet, but I feel they're being

Paths of Faith

answered as my spiritual consciousness evolves and expands.

What was it about Islam that made you think it would be the path that led you to find these answers?

I keep saying that it was the mystical stream of Sufism that first brought me to Islam, and that's true. From there I went into the more traditional aspects of Islam, but initially that was not the attraction for me. I had grown up in a religious tradition, and I wasn't really looking for a new religion. I was simply looking for the answers to the questions I had. The fact that the answers came through Bawa Muhaiyadeen, who was in the Islamic tradition, was what eventually led me to explore Islam itself. Once I was introduced to it and began studying it, I found that there were many beautiful things within it that I liked very much, and still do.

What kinds of things?

I love the prayers. I love the idea that without any kind of intermediary, without a priest or a pastor or anyone, five times a day I can do my ablutions in a very prayerful way and make the affirmation that I am about to enter into the presence of God and offer my prayers. When I do that, whether it's in my home or in a mosque or outside on a beach, I know that I am in communication with the Lord of the worlds, with the creator of the worlds, with my own creator. I love the notion that I am a divine spark from the creator, that I am a ray from the soul of God that has taken on a physical form for a period of time to learn certain things. Prayer time for me is very beautiful and very holy, and that is the thing I love most about Islam.

I also like the fasting. I love the fact that once a year thousands of communities of people around the world commit to a fast and commit to a heightened focus on our relationship with God, putting aside even our most basic desires (for food and drink) for a period of time as a discipline. We also fast as a means of purification and also as a way to feel the pangs of hunger in our own body and know what that means to many, many people in the world who are hungry every day even though it is not something they choose to do or be. So the fast is another of the five duties of the Muslim that I love very much.

I have also been fortunate to make the pilgrimage to Mecca. I have made what is called the *umra*, or the small pilgrimage, which is when you go to Mecca at any time other than the specific time of the year known as hajj. That was a wonderful experience. To actually be on the road from Medina to Mecca that was traveled by the Prophet and some of the disciples was very life changing. I saw how rugged and harsh the terrain there is, and I imagined what it must have been like fleeing into that desert on foot.

The other thing about the *umra* that was so wonderful was to look around the mosque in Mecca and see every race, every nationality, every color represented there. There were people wearing traditional dress from their countries, and we were all there together, bowing in unison to our creator. I was overwhelmed with the wonder of it, and the amazement. Anytime I was in that mosque, there would be at least a half million to a million people in it. That was an amazing sight. And after the prayers the women kiss the women, and the men kiss the men. Embracing and kissing on both cheeks women from all parts of the world, most of whom I could not speak to but with whom I shared a common language of prayer, was so beautiful. The prayers are all done in Arabic, and the greeting we give one another after prayer is in Arabic. Despite our different native languages, we said these things to one another in the same language. That prayer time in Mecca with people from all over the world became another bond that I made with Islam.

Was it those kinds of experiences that initially made you decide to fully convert, rather than just learn about Islam or practice certain parts of it?

In my case I did come to Islam because of the wisdom teachings of Sufism, which then made me look at the larger religion that they were a mystical aspect of. I don't think I would have done it the other way around. I don't think I would have been attracted initially to the traditional religion called Islam. I had to come in the door that I came in. But once I entered that door, and received an interpretation of Islam that was not focused on the legalistic aspects of Islam that form the more traditional view of the religion, but rather its beautiful spiritual and mystical aspects, I was able to see Islam as a whole in a different way.

Did that make it easier to accept parts of the religion you might have had trouble with otherwise?

Absolutely. I'm an activist. I became a student activist in high school. I dropped out of college to work full-time in the civil rights movement in Mississippi. I went against my parents, who were outraged that I gave up school for that. But I had to follow my own path. So I have never been a conformist in any way, and that was true of my approach to religion as well. It's really something for me to be in a religion that, if one chooses to live it that way, has some real serious rules and regulations. That would ordinarily not be in any way attractive to me. I would find it terribly confining if I were doing it only because some book or some teacher told me to do it. I had to see the benefit of it for myself and for other people, and I did that first, before I committed to it. I know very clearly that the prayers benefit me, and that the fast benefits me. I'm not doing these things because someone has told me they are what I have to do to be Muslim. I do them because I see that they work for me. I made the pilgrimage to see that in this particular tradition we have brotherhood and sisterhood with millions of people from around the world.

Looking at the Islamic laws and how they were formulated, as part of my dissertation work, also has a lot to do with how I am able to accept or live with the parts of Islam I have trouble with. I very much want to understand how much of these laws is made by human beings and how much came through revelation from God. What I find is that when it comes to the laws, a great deal of it is constructed by human beings, particularly men. It's a very patriarchal religion, and there's a reason for that. It was formed during a time when there was not even any question about the rightness of patriarchy. I do happen to be one of these women within the tradition of Islam who is questioning some of the laws of the religion, and feeling that it's important for Muslims to understand how the laws came to be. When you understand where the schools of law came from, and why, I think it becomes clear that there is a need for a reevaluation of them and, in some cases, a revision of them. This is not in any way a popular perspective.

How important do you think it is for people to do that, to reexamine the foundations of their beliefs and see how they came to be?

Gwendolyn Zoharah Simmons 225

I think that people need to study and look with wisdom and reason at the foundations of their beliefs. They need to use their reasoning power, their intellect, and their wisdom to understand, and not to do anything blindly. You must have some understanding of what you're doing in terms of religion. You must understand why you are in the religion and question what that religion is doing for you. Ask what its history is and what its purpose is. This is something I very much recommend doing, and it's one of the reasons that I teach religion. It's important that people not act like robots when it comes to following a religion. They need to take an active role in exploring their faith.

How long did that process of first learning about Islam to actually deciding to convert take for you?

I started studying with my teacher in 1971. I took the *shahadah* with him without having a real heart commitment to it. I had a commitment to my teacher, but it didn't mean that in my heart there had been a conversion. That process took some time. I would say that didn't take place until the early 1980s. So it was a long time. I went back to graduate school to study Islam really because I wanted to find out where it all came from and what it all meant, and I wanted to do it at a secular school because I wanted a non-theological perspective on it. I wanted a historical, sociological, and philosophical education related to the religion so that I could separate out the various components and see what about Islam I could embrace.

What were some of the hardest things to overcome in choosing to embrace it?

The role of women, of course, was very difficult for me. I considered, and still consider, myself a feminist. I have been active in the women's movement, which was a direct offshoot of my civil rights work. I had difficulty with the stereotypical view of the role of women within Islam and within those cultures we call Islamic societies. I had to study that and understand where it came from before I could embrace Islam. I needed to know if the problems I saw facing women were actually required by the religion, or if they were created by the way that people had interpreted the religion. This was a big issue for me. Until recently, women did not play significant roles in the leadership of Islam, and I had always been a person who took on leadership roles in whatever group I was in, whether it was my church or school or work. In the community founded by my teacher, women do have leadership roles. But in the larger Islamic community, that is often not encouraged, and it bothered me. To some extent it still does. It's not as if I've gotten over it. But my study of Islam has shown me that these problems are a result of human interpretation, and not of the religion itself.

Gwendolyn Zoharah Simmons   227

How were you able to separate your feelings about those issues from your love of what Islam was providing you?

That is a direct result of how I came into the religion. Sheikh Bawa Muhaiyadeen, the person with whom I studied, was the most kind and gentle human being I have ever met. He was adamant that there should be no compulsion in any religion, and especially in Islam. It is written in the Koran that no one has the right to make anyone do anything when it comes to religion and spirituality. It is completely anathema to Islam. These people who run around thinking they have the right, often at gunpoint, to make others pray or dress a certain way, or do anything they don't want to, are so far removed from what Islam teaches that they have nothing to do with what it is. I don't care how they present themselves or what authority they claim. They have nothing to do with true Islam. It's all about being power hungry and being after something other than spirituality.

Does it bother you that there are people in Islam who look at you and say you aren't really following the teachings of Islam because of your beliefs?

That happens quite often. For example, I do not dress in the way many Muslim women do. I do not cover my head in everyday life. I feel I dress modestly, but I do not wear a long robe or anything. I do cover my head when I go into a mosque, because to me that is a symbol of respect for God. But as far as my daily activities go, I don't dress in what would be called an Islamic fashion, and I have had numerous people speak to me about the "incorrectness" of that.

I am very concerned about what I call fundamentalism, or what some people call Islamism, which is espoused by many Islamic groups, including groups in the United States. Fundamentalists say that there is only one way to truly practice a religion, and of course they insist that it's their way. I see this as a real problem within the tradition, and within many religious traditions other than Islam. Basically it's a position taken by people seeking political power and has nothing to do with spirituality. It's an obsession with laws and with keeping other people under control, and I'm very concerned about it.

Is it ever tempting to give up on Islam because of those people and maybe go to another tradition where your views are more accepted?

There are a number of things that keep me in Islam. I have a wonderful community—the Bawa Muhaiyadeen Fellowship—I am involved with, and that is very important to me. It's my home base. Now, when I go to some other communities, I sometimes don't feel as comfortable. I try my best not to upset people by my presence or with my views, but if there is occasion for discussion, I will take part and say what I believe. I think those of us

Gwendolyn Zoharah Simmons   229

who have a human rights, civil rights, women's rights background are very much needed within the tradition to try in whatever ways we can to educate people about issues they might not otherwise think about. There are a lot of people in Islam who have been taught misinformation. Islam, like Judaism, is a religion based on law. Many people who come to Islam, and even those raised in it, are taught that these are divine laws. People get the idea that God handed them down on tablets or something. They are not, of course. They are laws made by men who have interpreted divine revelation. But unless people are encouraged to explore these things for themselves, they aren't going to know that. My work, the years I've put into learning the original language and studying the origins of Islam, is all done so that I can understand how many of the tenets and laws of the religion evolved, the role that interpretation played, and perhaps share that with others who have an interest. The laws were written by men who, to be fair, did the best they could given the times they were living in. But we are in a different time, and we can begin to interpret the Koran anew in light of the advances in thought and understanding of our day. We have to attempt to bring the laws into the modern age without losing sight of the core values of the religion. Thankfully there are a number of people trying to do this. Often they are treated badly for doing so, but they are continuing this work in spite of the opposition. I see myself as joining with that group and attempting to bring the interpretations and understanding of Islamic texts and traditions into our present-day knowledge.

You mentioned earlier that your study of mysticism made you realize that many mystic traditions share similar goals. Do you think that when it comes down to it, all religions are looking for the same thing?

I'm very involved in interreligious dialogue, and I'm comfortable in many different religious settings. I think this is because the light that we all seek in our practices is all one. It's we humans, my Sufi master taught, who have created religions and divided ourselves up into races and religions and used those as ways to hurt one another and to hate one another. But the light that we all seek is one.

FOR MORE INFORMATION

ON-LINE RESOURCES

Discover Islam
www.discoverislam.com

This entertaining Web site is built around a set of twenty-five posters, each of which presents information on a different aspect of Islamic religion and life.

Muslims Online
www.muslimsonline.com

Gwendolyn Zoharah Simmons   231

A collection of links and information of interest to the Muslim community and those looking for more information about Islam.

IslamiCity
www.islam.org

This site contains information about the Koran and Islamic teachings, as well as up-to-date news about issues of interest to the Islamic community.

BOOKS

Daughters of Another Path: Experiences of American Women Choosing Islam, by Carol Anway (Yawna Publications, 1995). In this book the author discusses her experiences as a mother whose daughter became a Muslim convert and the issues that resulted from it. The book also features short selections from fifty-three American-born women who have chosen to become Muslim, discussing why and how they came to Islam, what their lives are like as a result of that choice, and how non-Muslims can relate to Muslims who are family, friends, co-workers, and acquaintances.

Muhammad: A Biography of the Prophet, by Karen Armstrong (HarperSanFrancisco, 1993). This is a readable account of the life of the founder of Islam, written by a non-Muslim with respect for the tradition.

The Essential Koran, by Thomas Cleary (Books Sales, 1998). There are several excellent translations of the entire Koran. This volume includes selected readings from the holy book of Islam and is designed to help non-Muslims understand this sacred text.

Islam: The Straight Path, by John L. Esposito (Oxford University Press, 1998). Written for those interested in studying the Islamic faith in greater detail, this book outlines the beliefs of the religion and discusses Islamic society.

Islam: The Path of God, by Suzanne Haneef (Kazi Publications, 1997). An easy-to-understand explanation of Islam for anyone interested in the religion.

Islam (Teach Yourself World Faiths series), by Ruqaiyyah Waris Maqsood (Hodder & Stoughton, 1995). An introduction to Islam, written by a Muslim, for those interested in teaching themselves the basic beliefs of the religion.

Introducing Muhammad, by Ziauddin Sardar and Zafar Abbas Malik (Totem Books, 1994). A complete introduction to Islam, its founder, and the various issues that shape Islamic life and culture.

Gwendolyn Zoharah Simmons   233

Reverend Troy Perry

Founder, Universal Fellowship of Metropolitan Community Churches

"There are so many people who believe that because they are gay or lesbian, God created them so they could be hated by a culture that doesn't understand them. And that is not what God ever said."

One of the most difficult experiences faced by people following a spiritual path is when what they believe comes into conflict with what they are being taught by their faith. This is particularly true for people who are lesbian and gay. Because many religions have historically not been accepting of gay and lesbian people, many homosexuals have felt that there was no place for them in religion.

Over the years gay people have dealt with this situation in different ways. Some have abandoned religion altogether after being treated badly by the faiths they were part of. Some have chosen to remain in their faiths

234

despite not being officially accepted by them. Others have worked to change the opinions of their faiths, with varying degrees of success. Today some churches openly welcome lesbian and gay people into their congregations. Others continue to teach that there is no place for gay people in their traditions.

Reverend Troy Perry is one of those gay people who discovered that his beliefs did not match those of the church he was raised in. As a result, he left his church and began a new one. Founded in 1969, the Metropolitan Community Church is an evangelical Christian church that has become home to many gay men and lesbians, who find in it a welcoming, affirming place to worship. While the church membership is predominantly lesbian and gay, it is not exclusively so, and it is open to believers from many different traditions. Today there are more than three hundred MCC congregations around the world.

What kind of spiritual tradition were you raised in?

The majority of my father's family were Pentecostal, and the majority of my mother's family were Southern Baptist. In the South never the twain shall meet, so to speak. But in my home they did. My parents, typical of many parents in some ways, sent their children to church but did not always go with us. But I was one of those kids who genuinely enjoyed church.

What did you like about it?

With the Southern Baptists I loved their emphasis on Scripture. They had youth groups where we learned about the Bible, and they had Sunday school. With the Pentecostals I loved their exuberance. You could show emotion in their churches. You could clap your hands in church. People would cry in church. They would laugh in church. They permitted every emotion that a person has to be shown in church. The Baptists were different. They were very quiet.

I knew, too, somehow, that the church would affect my life forever. I knew it beyond a shadow of a doubt. There was something there that called me, and that's the only way I can describe it. Everybody views religion in a different way. But I knew that my life, whatever it became, would revolve around church.

What was your first experience working within the church?

It happened at age thirteen. I had felt for some time that God had called me in my heart and my mind. Then when I was twelve, my father was killed in an automobile wreck. I deeply loved my dad, and that was a very emotional time. A few months after that I was visiting my aunts and uncles in southern Georgia. It was while I was there that things began to happen. I'd had my conversion experience in the Baptist tradition—what we call accepting Jesus as our personal Lord and Savior—when I was ten years old. But then at thirteen I received what in the Pentecostal tradition we call the baptism of the Holy Spirit. Right after that happened, I felt a call to ministry, which I announced to my aunt, who was a Pentecostal pastor.

What was her response to hearing this from such a young person?

She immediately invited me to preach in the little church she pastored in. From that point I started preaching anywhere I had a chance to. Then I returned to Florida, where I lived with my mother. She was still a Baptist, so I once again started attending the Baptist Church with her. And at age fifteen I was licensed to preach in the Southern Baptist Church as well.

What did that mean?

It meant that the church recognized that I had a call to ministry. They understood and saw that for me preaching was very important. I also preached at my junior high school every Wednesday morning. I would end up with about two hundred kids who would come out to hear me preach, as well as some of my school-teachers.

Reverend Troy Perry

As a young person who had gone through two clearly influential conversion experiences, how did you see God?

I saw God as someone who loved me. God was a divine parent to me through Jesus Christ. My tradition—the Christian tradition—believes that Jesus came to Earth to live and die for us, and then rose from the dead. Jesus is very special to us. As a young man I believed with all my heart that Jesus could do anything to help me. I also believed that I was to carry the good news of Jesus to all the world. Whenever I had a problem, I would just stop and pray. This gave me a lot of comfort and a lot of satisfaction. Now, I joke and say that without prayer I would never have made it through school. But what I learned was that God expected me to put legs on my prayers. I couldn't just pray to pass a test without studying for it. But if I studied *and* I prayed, it seemed to work for me every time.

How did the other kids you were preaching to respond to you?

It was a mixed bag. Most of my friends in school were also from my church, so they understood it. And there were people who had the utmost admiration for what I did, including some of my teachers. Others, I'm sure, viewed me as a little fanatic. But I knew that I was doing what I felt was right, and for me that was

Paths of Faith

enough. I felt that God loved me, and that was what was important.

Did you have any idea then that you might be gay?

The Sunday school songs like "Jesus Loves Me" and "Jesus Loves the Little Children" told us that Jesus loved all the children in the world, regardless of color or differences. I always believed the words of those songs. But the minute I went through puberty, and all at once was faced with sexual feelings toward other boys, I ran into problems. The church in the 1950s didn't talk about homosexuality. But they talked about people who were "led astray" by their sexuality. That really bothered me. As a teenager, like most teenagers, I dealt with the issue of masturbation. Well, nobody ever said in our tradition it was a sin to masturbate, but they made it sound like it was not something good for us to do. I used to pray to God and say, "Please stop me if you don't want me to do this." God just didn't seem to answer that prayer. My sex drive was still there. So I had problems, especially around the feelings I had toward people of the same sex. As I came more and more to terms with what this meant, then I started trying to figure out what to do and how to get over it.

Did you think being gay was something you could just get rid of?

Reverend Troy Perry   239

When I was sixteen, I went into a public library in Mobile, Alabama, and was reading about Greek mythology. In those stories I saw that there were men who loved men, and I just couldn't get over that. And I couldn't believe that these men who loved other men were actually heroes, because in the depths of my heart my church was sending me a different message about sex. Then I found a book on psychology, and when I opened it, the word *homosexual* was in there. That book said three things about homosexuals. First, they were sick. Second, every homosexual wanted to go to bed with little boys. And third, every homosexual wanted to wear his mother's dresses. I slammed the book shut, thinking, "Thank God I'm not sick." I didn't want to wear my mama's dresses and I didn't want to sleep with little boys. So I didn't think being homosexual applied to me.

But your feelings were still going against what the church told you. How did you deal with that?

In 1956 there were not good things being written about gay people. So I didn't know what to do with the conflicting information I had. When I was eighteen, I went to the pastor of my Pentecostal church and tried to tell him about what I called the "funny feelings" I was having. That's the only way I could describe it. Finally, after an hour, his eyes lit up and he said, "Oh, I know what you need to do. You just need to marry a good woman, and that will take care of all those feelings."

So did you?

I took his advice and I married his daughter.

But wasn't that difficult, as you were sexually interested in men?

Well, remember that we were both part of the church, and the church taught that you weren't to have any sort of sexual contact with a woman if you weren't married. When we were dating, we dated by going to church. The church didn't permit us to dance or to drink or to go to movies or to do much of anything else. So it was very easy. We would go and sit in the front row of the church, where her father could keep an eye on us.

Did she have any idea that you were gay?

She had some idea because her father had talked to her about it a little bit. I tried to talk to her about it, but we didn't know how to. So we graduated from high school and decided to get married before I went on to Bible college. We married and then headed for Illinois, where I was enrolled in Bible school.

Reverend Troy Perry

Did your feelings about men indeed go away, as you hoped?

No, they just continued on. I prayed for deliverance, but they would not go away.

Did you think that perhaps God was testing your faith in the way that the Bible says he tested many of his followers in the Old Testament?

I didn't know why God would do this to me. I didn't know why the God that I knew would say, "I made you this way, but now you're not allowed to act on it." That seemed like a horrible thing to me. So I kept praying and kept trying to do my best, but it was very difficult. I was having a relationship with my wife, but I felt very empty inside. That's the only way I can describe it.

What finally forced you to face the reality of your gayness?

About five years after I was married, I was pastoring a Pentecostal church in California. I went into a bookstore to buy a copy of *Time* magazine because there was an article in it that I wanted to quote from in a sermon. As I was looking around I saw what we used to call physique magazines, magazines with photos of bodybuilders. Looking at those magazines, I realized that I had to stop running from what and who I was. I walked up to the woman behind the counter and I said, "Do you

Paths of Faith

have any books about homosexuality?" She looked me up and down, which made me very nervous, and said that she did have a few. I asked for a copy of every book she had, and I remember that I wrote out a check for $18.21 for them.

I took the books back to the parsonage and started reading them. And it was while I was reading them that I discovered the woman had stuck two things into the bag. One was a book called *The Homosexual in America*, by Donald Webster Cory, and once I read that book, I knew what I was feeling was not the end of the world, and that I could be myself as a gay man and live a productive life. And the other thing she put in was a copy of a little magazine called *One*, which was one of the first gay magazines. That let me know there were millions of people just like me. The morning after I read those books, I got up and went into the bathroom to shave. While I was shaving, I stopped, looked in the mirror, and said out loud, "Troy Perry, you're a homosexual." It was like a third born-again experience. I broke down crying, not because I felt bad but because I felt so good.

But you still had your church to worry about.

I still had my church, and I also had my wife and our two children. I had no idea what was going to happen. But I knew that I had to be who I was. With that, I went to see our district overseer, the head of our church. I told him about my feelings. He turned blue in the face and asked me if I'd molested anyone in the Sunday school, which of course I hadn't. When I explained that I had read these books and that I knew I was a homosexual, he said, "This is just a trick of the devil. We're going to pray about it." So we prayed. Then he told me to rip up the books and keep praying. But I told him that I'd been praying for a long time and that it wasn't going to work. I told him I knew I was gay and hoped that he would inform the bishop of the church when he next saw him.

And did he?

He sure did. A month later I was excommunicated from the Pentecostal Church for being a homosexual.

Did that make you bitter about religion?

No, it didn't. It made me very sad. My attitude was, "Okay, God. You can't love me and I can't love you. At least that's what the church has told me. They've said that I can't be gay and be Christian. So don't bug me and I won't bug you." Today I know that is *not* how God works, but I thought then it was my only choice. And I was very sad, because church meant so much to me.

All you knew was a life in the church. What did you do now that you couldn't have that?

Shortly after being excommunicated, my wife and I separated, and I moved to Los Angeles and started discovering the gay community. I found other people like me. Then within eighteen months I was drafted into the U.S. Army. When I went into the military, I kept looking for church. I didn't cut myself off completely from church.

Did the military know you were gay?

Oh, yes. Once I had come to terms with being a gay person, that was it for me. I knew that good, bad, or indifferent, it was the life I would lead for the rest of my life, and I was determined never to back down for a minute from being who I was. I told them that I was gay. But it was the Vietnam War, and they needed people. America has always done that. In wartime they don't care what you are. But when the war is over, then they separate you out and say you aren't fit to serve. I had a top secret clearance. I would have died for my country. But I was openly gay in my unit.

Did you find what you were looking for in terms of spirituality in the army?

The town where I was stationed in Germany had a Pentecostal church, and I went there. But when my two

Reverend Troy Perry   245

years were up, I came home still struggling with the conflict between religion and who I was. It just would not let me go. And then I fell deeply, madly in love for the first time in my life. While I cared for my wife, the intensity I felt for this man who came into my life was nothing like that.

How did he influence your life?

We were together for six months. Then he left, and I went into a deep depression. Nobody seemed to want to talk to me about what I was feeling. Worst of all, I felt that I couldn't talk to God about it, because we'd made a bargain not to bother each other. So I got in the bathtub, turned on the water, and cut both of my wrists with a razor blade. I just wanted to die. My roommate came home, heard the water running, and broke down the door. He got me to the hospital.

It sounds like things were going from bad to worse.

Well, God works in mysterious ways. Because something happened to me in the hospital that changed my life forever. I was there in the hospital room with bandages on my arms, waiting for the doctor to come in and sew me back up. All at once a woman walked into the room. She walked over to me and said, "I don't know why you've done this. This is really crazy. But I want to tell you, I've tried it too." She held out her arms, and the scars there were unbelievable. Then she said, "I went on and I made something of myself." She kept talking to me, and she said, "There's got to be *somebody* you can talk to. Can't you just look up and talk to God?"

This woman pushed every one of my buttons, especially those about church. Her statement about looking up to God made me break down all over again. I was just sobbing. She left the room, and I prayed. I said, "God, I want to ask forgiveness for something. Not for being gay, but for turning this man, my lover, into God. And when he fell, I ended up here." I had committed the sin talked about in Romans 1:26–28—not the sin of homosexuality, but the sin of worshiping the creature more than the creator. I asked forgiveness for that, and afterward I felt a joy that I hadn't felt in years.

Did that joy stay with you after you left the hospital, or was it a momentary thing?

After the doctor sewed up my wrists, I went home. The next day I was lying in bed thinking about everything that had happened. I still felt that joy, but it confused me. I thought, "This can't be God. I'm still a homosexual, and that won't change. God, you can't love me." And God spoke to me in that still small voice in my mind and said, "Troy, I love you. You're my son. So don't tell me what I can and can't do." At that

Reverend Troy Perry   247

moment I knew that I *could* be gay and be a Christian.

And did that send you back to the church?

Well, I started looking for a church to go to. But I still couldn't find one that would take me as I was. Then I started dating a young man. One night we went to a gay bar. While we were there, two undercover police officers arrested my date and one of my best friends on a made-up charge. My date had patted my friend on the butt while saying hello to him, and the police said that they had engaged in lewd behavior. So they arrested them. Remember, this was in the 1960s, before the Stonewall riots and the gay rights movement. This kind of thing happened all the time.

And how did this affect your spiritual search?

When my friends were taken to the police station, the policeman kept telling my friend Tony that they were going to call his employer and tell them about the arrest. He was terrified that he would lose his job because he was gay. He said, "If there's anything I've learned, it's that nobody likes a queer." I felt horrible. I said, "People do care. And even if they don't, God cares." Tony laughed in my face and said, "Troy, God doesn't care about me. I went to my priest when I was fifteen years old, and he ordered me out of the church because he was afraid I would contaminate other kids. No, Troy, God doesn't care about me."

After I took him home and went back to my own house, I knelt and prayed. I said, "God, you know I've been looking for a place to attend church and haven't found one. If you want to see a church started as a special outreach into the gay and lesbian community, but with its doors open to all, then just let me know." And again that still small voice in my mind said, "Do this now."

How did you start?

I put up a poster in the local gay dance bar. I can't imagine that happening now, but back then that's how the community got news out. The bar owner was very supportive. He even stopped the music one night to announce the service. People looked at me like I was nuts. I also took out an ad in the *Advocate*, the gay newspaper. At first they didn't want to take it, but I sat with the owners of the paper and told them my dream, and when I was done, they gave me the space. So I put in the ad, giving people my name and my home address. I set the date of the first service for October 6, 1968.

When you placed the ad, what did you think the response would be?

All my friends thought I was insane. They kept telling me that the police were going to raid the service, because at the time things like that still occurred. But I said, "God has told me to do this." My biggest fear was that people would come the first time but then wouldn't come back the second Sunday. That's every preacher's biggest fear!

Did people come?

I didn't know if anyone would come except my roommate, who had promised to be there. But at that first service we had twelve people—nine friends and three strangers. Among the attendees there was one woman, one person of color, one Jewish person, and one heterosexual couple. It was a mix of people, and I always say it was a vision of things to come.

What was it like to see your dream come true?

That first day was mind-boggling. The two most wonderful things for me were the music—we had tape-recorded the Mormon Tabernacle Choir so we could sing along with that—and when we took Communion. That's when I knew we were part of something historic. When I called for the Communion, only three people came forward. But everybody in the room was crying watching it. Then once service was over, it was like the room was filled with the buzzing of bees as everyone talked about how wonderful it had been.

And did the church grow?

It grew every week after that, except for the fourth week, when it dropped to nine attendees and I thought I would die. But that Sunday, after I spoke, someone came up to me and said, "You preached like there were a thousand people here." And I said, "There will be." Within a year and a half we were running over a thousand in attendance, and we had our own property in Los Angeles.

When you started, did you feel like you were starting it to meet your own personal needs, or did you always see it as something for the larger community?

I probably needed it more than anybody else. It was like God was wrestling with me and not letting me go until I did it. But I knew immediately, after the first few services, that there were many other people who had the same hunger and yearning for spirituality that I did. As we started growing I started receiving mail from all over the world about people's spiritual needs and about needing a church like ours. That's when I knew God was going to use us greatly and mightily around the world, and that there was a deep hunger for spirituality within the gay and lesbian community. There were a lot of people who, like me, had thrown the baby out with the bathwater. And I knew that they didn't have to do that.

Reverend Troy Perry   251

I always tell gay and lesbian people in my situation one thing: "God did not create you so that he could have someone to sit around and hate." That's one of the things I have to battle with constantly. There are so many people who believe that because they are gay or lesbian, God created them so they could be hated by a culture that doesn't understand them. And that is not what God ever said.

How do you define the Metropolitan Community Church?

I view it as an evangelical, liturgical, ecumenical church. That does not mean that everyone involved with MCC is evangelical. We have liberals and we have conservatives. People come into our churches from all kinds of denominations, and we make it work. The people in our congregations bring with them all of the good things from the traditions they've come out of, and we use those things. Those things that are not so good, we don't use. But we have respect for other traditions, and we are not going to have fistfights over what our past denominations are. Everybody is welcome, even seekers who can't even call themselves Christians yet. We encourage them to come and see what answers they find here.

So the details of how you worship are not the primary focus?

No, it's all about personal experience. We believe that everybody has to work out his or her own salvation with fear and trembling. Maybe God will speak to you in one way and give you things that you can do that other people can't do. And maybe other people have gifts that you don't have. That's not what you should worry about. Your business is your relationship to God through Jesus Christ.

Do you believe that there is special power in gay people coming together as a special, united church, or do you think that gay people can stay within other traditions—even ones that don't accept them—and find answers there?

I believe that gay people can come to our churches and find incredible power. I believe that gay people can go to the other churches, where they are a minority, and that God will bless them and anoint them there. If they're happy there, then they should stay with those churches. But I also think there's special power in gay people coming together to worship. I had someone come to me who had been part of what we call an affirming church, a church that welcomes lesbian and gay people. He said, "Reverend Perry, in my church we celebrated gay pride once a year. Here you celebrate it every Sunday." And there is power in that.

Do you see MCC as a "gay church"?

I tell people that we are the church of Jesus Christ. When I founded the church, I did it as a special outreach into the gay and lesbian community, but I wanted to keep its doors open to everybody. We have everybody in MCC. We have heterosexuals. We have bisexuals. We have family groups. We have singles and couples. You name it, and we have it in MCC. So I think it's true to say we are a gay church if it's said in the same way that someone would call something a black church, or a Hispanic church, where it's founded as a special coming together of a particular church but it's still available to everyone.

Over the years you've had, not surprisingly, a lot of negative response from some in the religious community who think what you're doing is totally wrong. Do you think that whole argument even matters?

Not anymore. It really doesn't. There are some people in MCC who take it much more seriously than I do. But I just can't take those people who don't like us seriously anymore. I think it's a dead issue. Now, having said that, I have to say that in many cultures it is still a *very* serious issue. There are cultures that are so homophobic that religion still plays a major role in oppressing gay people. The Anglican Church in places like Africa or Asia, for instance, is very intolerant of gay and lesbian people, even though the Episcopal Church here in America is mostly welcoming. So you have to look at where you are. We have MCC churches all over the world, so of course we do deal with that. But for the most part I don't worry about people from the Religious Right.

Does it bother you when people still try to tell you that you aren't really a Christian because you're gay and because, in their interpretation, the Bible says that's wrong?

The Bible tells me that if I confess with my mouth that Jesus Christ is Lord and believe in my heart that God has raised him from the dead, then I will be saved. It doesn't say that other people can stand between God and me and tell me anything different. It says that if I do that, then I am saved. It doesn't require anything else from anybody else, especially their opinions.

Could you have ever imagined that your life would turn out as it has?

To be honest, no. I've lived the most interesting life in the world. I'm eternally grateful to God. Thirty years ago I had people spit in my face because of what I was doing. Now look at where we are. It's been an incredible faith journey.

Through it all has your view of God changed?

Not at all, other than it's grown stronger and stronger. I'm eternally grateful to God. I just want to know in my heart of hearts that when the time comes

Reverend Troy Perry   255

for God to call me home, I have been faithful. If I know that, I will die a very, very happy man.

Many people get so caught up in following the rules of their various traditions that they find it hard to simplify things that way. How do you do that?

For me, Jesus said there are two rules to remember, and I live by them. The first is that you are to love the Lord thy God with all of your heart, your mind, and your strength. Second, you are to learn to love your neighbor as yourself. If I can do those two things, then everything else will follow.

And do you still get as much joy out of it as you did when you began all of this at the age of thirteen?

Even more. The one thing I absolutely adore is being able to speak, to teach, and to do what God called me to do as a boy. I am eternally thankful that I continue to have that in my life. And I would say to any young person who feels a call to ministry that it is a life of utter joy. If you really are called, and you always ask God what it is he wants you to do in your life, and you are open to doing exactly what God says, you will have a wonderful life.

What about those young people who, like yourself, feel that they aren't what God wants them to be because their traditions or other people are telling them that?

They honestly have to separate out what it is God wants from them from what the world wants. And you get that not only by listening to what people say to you, but by listening to and finding God in your heart and in your life. You find it by studying the word of God as it is revealed to you, and not to other people. People ask me if I take the Bible literally, and I always tell them, "No, I take it seriously." Taking the word of God seriously is different, because it means that you find out who it was written to, why it was written that way, and what it means to us today.

FOR MORE INFORMATION

ON-LINE RESOURCES

Universal Fellowship of Metropolitan Community Churches
www.ufmcc.org

This site contains information about Metropolitan Community Church activities and its many member churches across the United States and around the world. It also contains links to other sites of interest, as well as links to other sites about gays and lesbians and religion.

Reverend Troy Perry

BOOKS

A great deal has been written about the issue of lesbian and gay people in the various churches. While Rev. Troy Perry's interview discusses gay people primarily in the Christian Church, there are lesbian and gay people in all religions. The following list contains books that are good places to begin if you're interested in learning more about how gay people are dealing with the issue of spirituality in their lives.

Twice Blessed: On Being Lesbian, Gay, and Jewish, edited by Christie Balka and Andy Rose (Beacon Press, 1991). This collection of essays by gay men and women exploring their Jewish heritage and faith was one of the first books to address the issue, and it continues to be one of the best.

Wrestling with the Angel: Faith and Religion in the Lives of Gay Men, edited by Brian Bouldrey (Riverhead Books, 1996). This book features twenty-one essays by gay men from a range of spiritual traditions discussing the issues they have faced in exploring their faith.

What the Bible Really Says about Homosexuality, by Daniel A. Helminiak (Alamo Square Press, 1994). This comprehensive yet easily understood book is the classic text in the debate over what the church teaches about lesbians and gay men.

Don't Be Afraid Anymore: The Story of Reverend Troy Perry and the Metropolitan Community Churches, by Troy Perry (St. Martin's, 1992). The autobiography of the founder of the Metropolitan Community Church.

Is the Homosexual My Neighbor? A Positive Christian Response, by Letha Dawson Scanzoni and Virginia Ramey Mollenkott (HarperSanFrancisco, 1994). One of the earliest books to discuss the issue of the church's position on homosexuality, this book offers many helpful suggestions both for gay people and for straight people who want to understand more about the struggle lesbians and gay men face when it comes to religious issues.

Coming Out While Staying In: Struggles and Celebrations of Lesbians, Gays, and Bisexuals in the Church, by Leanne McCall Tiget (United Church Press, 1996). A collection of writings about how gay, lesbian, and bisexual women and men are finding their place within the church.

Stranger at the Gate: To Be Gay and Christian in America, by Mel White (Plume, 1995). Once regarded by the leaders of the conservative Religious Right as one of their most talented and productive supporters, evangelical minister Mel White shocked the religious community when he revealed his homosexuality. This autobiography details his long struggle to accept himself and to find a place in a church that tried to drive him away.

Reverend Troy Perry

About the Author

Michael Thomas Ford is the award-winning author of numerous works of fiction and nonfiction for adults and teenagers. His books for young adults include *Outspoken: Role Models from the Lesbian and Gay Community*, which was named an NCSS-CBC Outstanding Social Studies Trade Book and a *Booklist* Editors' Choice "Top of the Lists" selection, as well as *The Voices of AIDS* and *100 Questions and Answers About AIDS*, both of which were named American Library Association Best Books for Young Adults.